THE *W*EDDING *D*RESS DIET

THE WEDDING DRESS DIET

LOSE WEIGHT AND LOOK
GREAT ON YOUR WEDDING DAY
AND BEYOND

Robyn Flipse, R.D., and Jacqueline Shannon

MAIN STREET BOOKS
DOUBLEDAY
New York London Toronto Sydney Auckland

A Main Street Book
Published by Doubleday, a division of Random House, Inc., 1540
Broadway, New York, New York 10036

MAIN STREET BOOKS, DOUBLEDAY, and the portrayal of a building
with a tree are trademarks of Doubleday, a division of Random House, Inc.

Cataloging-in-Publication Data is on file with the Library of Congress.

FIRST EDITION

Designed by Claudyne Bianco-Bedell

Illustrated by Sandra Bruce

ISBN 0-385-49901-9

00 01 02 03 04 10 9 8 7 6 5 4 3 2 1

ROBYN FLIPSE:

To my son, Peter Samuel Flipse Dorian

JACQUELINE SHANNON:

To my daughter, Madeline Maria Trobaugh

$\mathcal{A}$CKNOWLEDGMENTS

$\mathcal{T}$n my 25-year career as a Registered Dietitian I have held many challenging and diversified positions in my chosen profession. When I reflect on all of the jobs I have had, I feel fortunate to have found work that I so thoroughly enjoy. Someone who understood just how much I loved what I did for a living once said to me, "You got into the right occupation at the right time." I think he was right.

Writing *The Wedding Dress Diet* was another exciting opportunity for me. But as with most new ventures, it could not have happened without the encouragement and support of others who believed I had what it takes to write this book.

The person I am most indebted to for seeing an author behind the veneer of this registered dietitian is Linda Konner, my literary agent. Of Linda I can truly say, she read me like a book. Her thoughtful probing of my experience and abilities led her to believe I had what it takes. Then all she had to do was convince me! I am forever grateful she succeeded.

To Linda I must also credit the brilliant choice of coauthor, Jackie Shannon. From opposite coasts we worked together like the keys on the keyboards of our respective word processors. I know I could not have met our near impossible deadlines without her cheerful coaching in the wee hours of my mornings and her nights.

As for my expertise on brides and weddings, I must first acknowledge my four sisters—now, all married. I have had the privilege of playing a role in the day each of them took center stage, and have amassed a wealth of do's and don'ts from those shared family ceremonies.

Next I must recognize the innumerable clients whom I have helped as they counted down the days until their final fittings. To each I owe a debt of gratitude for teaching me so much about what it means to be your personal best on this very special day.

And then for up-to-the-minute highlights, I must thank my eldest son and his bride-to-be who were staging the very last-minute details of their wedding day as this manuscript was being sent off to the printer. I could not have asked for a more up-front and personal experience in the long days and nights that I wrote these chapters.

May you all live happily ever after.

—Robyn Flipse

ACKNOWLEDGMENTS

I'd like to add my thanks . . .

To Linda Konner: not just your traditional agent, but matchmaker, firefighter, cheerleader, and mother of great ideas as well!

To my coauthor Robyn, whose energy, organization, speed, and creativity constantly astonished and delighted me.

To Jennifer Griffin, our editor at Doubleday-Broadway, whose never-flagging enthusiasm, thoughtful and concise editing, and rapid turnarounds of our drafts belied the fact that she was juggling other books . . . as well as attending to the million details of her own wedding!

To my daughter Madeline, for the interest she takes in each one of my projects, to the point that—barely eleven years old—anecdotes and tidbits she collects through her own reading have ended up in every one of my nonfiction books, including this one.

To my "hang-in-there" friends, Dirk Sutro, Reggie Calvin, and Michael Vlassis.

And to Dr. Eugene J. Farmer, whose various contributions to my life since I became an adult go well beyond my own wedding. Thanks again, Dad.

—Jacqueline Shannon

$\mathcal{C}$ONTENTS

CONTENTS

THE WEDDING DRESS DIET

*asters * A host of subtle ways to cut fat and calories in your every-day cooking * Charting your weight on every anniversary * Some final words of wisdom*

ℐNTRODUCTION

WEDDING DRESS WOES

*T*wo weeks before her June 28th wedding, Jacy Johnson*, twenty-eight, went for the final fitting of her wedding dress. As she stood on a raised platform for the seamstress, Jacy was stunned to see that her stomach pooched out quite noticeably in the floor-length tube of a slip dress similar to the one worn by Carolyn Bessette Kennedy in her marriage to John F. Kennedy, Jr., a few years earlier.

Jacy called this to the attention of her mother and the seam-

---

* Name changed at her insistence!

stress. The seamstress clucked her tongue sympathetically. "You can always wear shapewear," she said, heading off to find what our mothers used to call a girdle so that Jacy could see just how much the pooch could be masked. The "tummy terminator" nearly took Jacy's breath away with its industrial-strength Lycra and stays. Worse, the pooch was still apparent.

Jacy's mother sighed heavily. "That's what you get for ordering a dress six months in advance."

"Like I had a choice," Jacy snapped, glaring at her mother. But when she got home and stepped on the scale, she knew her mother had a point. She'd packed on several pounds. She couldn't lay the blame entirely on the glasses of champagne she'd been lifting at various premarriage celebrations with her friends, or the rich sugary pastries, cream soups, and chocolate-dipped strawberries she'd scarfed at the bridal showers. Having had to run around seeing to all the details of her huge, elaborate wedding during her lunch hours as a corporate communications specialist at a San Diego–based company, Jacy was forced to opt for fast-food lunches or quick stops at 7-Eleven for microwaved hot dogs and burritos.

Well, Jacy vowed, this was war. She had two weeks to wage a pooch putsch. She did some research on the Internet, scanning the archives of women's magazines for diets that promised to help a reader doff ten pounds in two weeks or less. She settled on an extreme version of what's commonly known as the Dr. Atkins diet. She ate vast quantities of protein and some fat, but zero carbohydrates. For two weeks, Jacy downed nothing but meat and cheese. No carbs. No vegetables or fruit. Water weight poured off of her. She was constantly in the bathroom. Within eleven days, she'd lost eleven pounds. Two days before the wedding, however, she woke up with a painful, swollen tongue. It hurt to talk. It hurt to swallow. She visited her doctor. "It's either a virus that will go away in a few days, or your diet has been very poor," the doctor told her.

When her big day arrived, Jacy's tongue still hurt. She could barely find the energy to walk down the aisle wearing her ornate, heavy headdress. She was exhausted. She and her new husband had to leave their expensive, carefully planned reception much earlier than they'd expected. On her Hawaiian honeymoon, Jacy indulged herself in breads, rice, pasta, potatoes—all the carbs she'd been craving. She felt bloated on the beach in Maui and refused to let her new husband take pictures of her in her bikini. Back on the mainland, she discovered she'd regained every bit of the weight she had struggled to lose . . . and then some.

Jacy grins sheepishly when she relates this tale, then tells us a friend of hers—let's call her Lisa—can top it. Seems Lisa was so desperate to lose ten pounds in the week before her own wedding that she went to a seven-day, boot-camp-like "fasting" camp in which only water was served. By the fourth day, Lisa was so starving that she stole a packet of honey from the staff dining room and brushed her teeth with it, spitting it out so that the medical supervisors wouldn't catch on to her cheating.

Professionally, we, the authors, have heard dozens of similar horror stories—Robyn, as a registered dietitian who has maintained a thriving nutrition counseling practice since 1985, and Jacqueline, a long-time freelance health writer who not too long ago wrote both the health and diet columns in *Cosmopolitan* magazine.

The typical bride-to-be's desperate vow—"I must look *perfect* on my wedding day"—is a mantra we hear in our personal lives, as well. Within the last year, Robyn participated in two weddings—once as mother of the groom, once as sister of the bride. Jacqueline was twice a bridesmaid. Earlier in our lives, each of us was a bride. We know well that for every woman who has ever walked down the aisle or under a *huppah*, the size label sewn inside that wedding dress is a number that she lives with forever. (And she's got the photos and videotapes to prove it!) Years later, she may not remember the names of all of her bridesmaids, but she *will* remember whether she was a size six or a size sixteen as she took her vows.

And who can blame women for obsessing about looking the best they'll ever look at this pinnacle event? After all, a typical woman's wedding day is the one day in her life that she's guaranteed to be the star of the show, the center of attention, the person in the spotlight. All eyes will be on *her*.

Even celebrities who are accustomed to living their lives under the constant scrutiny of the public eye feel a special paranoia about their wedding day. In the weeks before her wedding to Great Britain's Prince Edward, Sophie Rhys-Jones, for example, underwent a bizarre treatment called a Frigi-Thalgo body wrap in order to help her lose twenty pounds. If you can believe the tabloid press, Sophie was "smeared with a foul-smelling seaweed concoction and then wrapped mummy-style in cold, wet bandages," according to the *Star*. Ugh! It's described as "a bit like sitting in your wet clothes after you come in from the rain." Except that you stink, too.

Sarah, the former Duchess of York, aka "Fergie" and Sophie's sister-in-law—or whatever you call their relationship in light of Fergie's divorce—recently rolled her eyes as she recalled the drastic steak-and-oranges diet she tried the month before her 1986 wedding. She rounded out those deadly boring diet meals with "injections and pills—and we're not talking vitamins, either," she said. "Your hair falls out and your skin's a mess, but you lose weight! I lost twenty-six pounds in four weeks."

Not long after, the five-foot, eight-inch duchess ballooned to 210 pounds.

Do we believe that women are far too hard on themselves when it comes to body image? Absolutely. Do we also accept the reality that almost all brides-to-be go on a diet? That, too. One of us—Robyn—can document the fact that prospective brides are the third-largest group of people (after athletes and pregnant women) concerned about their weight.

Our mission is this: With our safe and sane diet and exercise plan, we will help you, the soon-to-be-married woman, accomplish your weight-loss and shape-up goals without sacrificing your skin or your hair or your energy or your sanity for, say, your thunder thighs. In addition, our advice will keep your immune system healthy and strong so you can survive all of the stress of getting to the church on time.

The corollary to this is you will have the foundation for a varied and healthy eating style for life. You have probably heard the statistic that "95 percent of all diets fail." This is misleading; it implies you can't lose weight on a diet. The truth is that most people *do* lose weight when they go on a diet. But 95 percent of them put the weight back on within a year. That's mostly thanks to the rigidity and monotony of the majority of diets. Sure, you can eat nothing but steak and oranges for a couple of weeks—but think about staying on that diet for the next year. You couldn't. You would go absolutely mad. You would crave the forbidden so much that one day, like a rabid animal, you would wrestle that package of Wheat Thins from your new husband's hands and—cramming and snarling—eat the entire box without even bothering to sit down. Sooner rather than later, you would balloon just like Fergie, and you'd become a card-carrying member of the Ninety-five Percent Club.

That won't happen here. There is nothing monotonous about the Wedding Dress Diet. Our philosophy is that you can eat anything you want . . . *in moderation.* Moderation meaning that if you split a dish of chocolate mousse with your best friend at lunch, then don't have dessert after dinner. Because in our book, calories are king. It's not the proverbial end-all and be-all—Robyn is, after all, a dietitian with some very hardcore beliefs about good nutrition (as you'll learn in Chapter Four). But we live in the real world, too. We know the odds of finding a bag of baby carrots in your office vending machine as opposed to a Snickers bar or bag of Doritos. So you won't get a lot of finger wagging from us. You blow it occasionally? In our book, the day is still salvageable—you'll have no excuse to say, "Well, since I blew it at lunch I might as well go all out at dinner, too."

The Wedding Dress Diet is not monotonous, but it *is* rigid . . . especially if, like Fergie, you have only a blessed few weeks left till your big day. We are going to coach you to be hyperstrict about calories and exercising during the weeks or months you are dieting. You *have* to be, because unlike most dieters, you have a hard and fast deadline for losing the weight: your wedding day. What makes our plan special, however, is that *you* get to decide on the relative rigidity of your personal plan. We provide a simple formula to enable you to determine exactly how many calories you must limit yourself to eating each day and how much exercising you must do based on the weeks or months till your wedding and the number of pounds you want to lose. Another silver lining of the Wedding Dress Diet is that we give you lots and lots of tips and guidelines so that, even after you've reached your goal weight and can loosen up on your calorie and exercise quotas, you can eat deliciously and nutritiously while maintaining your weight loss forever and without feeling deprived or hungry or simply bored to death.

There are lots of other features in this diet book that make it so different from any other. For example:

- We'll help you cope with this unique predicament: While you may feel that, say, the four months you have remaining till your wedding is ample time to reach your goal weight, you may be stunned to discover that you must order your wedding gown at least four to six months in advance . . . that is, well before you achieve the body you want!

- With our chapter on selecting the right wedding dress, we will not leave out advice for you if, for whatever reason, you have not achieved the body you were hoping for before your wedding. With our suggestions on selecting the perfect neckline, skirt style, and so on, we will show you how to maximize your particular figure assets while minimizing those you're not happy with.

- We are also very democratic. We recognize that most of our readers will be first-time brides, but we don't forget the second-time-around bride. In our exercise chapter, for example, we address the needs of the woman who is working on her second wedding and who may not have much time or energy for working out because she may be juggling not just a top-flight career but a couple of kids, as well. Another example: In our chapter on selecting the perfect wedding dress, we don't stop at helping brides mask common but changeable problems, such as a protruding tummy, but those who have irreversible "flaws," as well, such as being very short in stature.

- Finally—and once again—we won't abandon you at the altar! Our book takes you well beyond your wedding day. We're providing not just simple, delicious ways to maintain your new figure for years to come, but also tips on such topics as how to indulge but not overdo it on your honeymoon and how to get your husband and your in-laws to adapt—or at least tolerate and support—your new healthy lifestyle.

Congratulations on your engagement. And now, let's go, girl.

CHAPTER ONE

TAKING STOCK

$\mathcal{A}$sk any woman if she is happy with her body and she will undoubtedly say "No," then proceed to list the usual figure flaws. But for a bride-to-be, figure flaws seem to become a matter of life or death. No one wants to walk down the aisle, all eyes upon her, with "thunder thighs," "a pot belly," and/or "flabby wings." Fortunately, no one has to.

By now you've probably figured out that the perfect wedding takes lots of time and heaps of planning. If so, you're making daily "to-do" lists and checking them twice. Fitting into the perfect gown takes the same strategy.

A series of fad diets interspersed with bouts of manic exercise will not help you get into shape for your big day or stay in shape for a minute after. You need a more personal approach to lose your unwanted pounds and firm those reluctant muscles.

If you are ready to commit to an eating and exercise overhaul, you will reap endless benefits. Try to think of the Wedding Dress Diet as a new part-time job. Yes, it's more work for you at a time when you're already super busy, but the payoff is also like a second income. You will look and feel great, and can continue to collect the dividends as long as you do the work.

As with any new job, there's some paperwork to complete. In this case, it is figuring out what your body measurements are now. Then you can follow the chapter-by-chapter instructions that will help you change your size and shape into something you'll be proud to have captured in all those wedding photos (some of which may crop up again—even in your local newspaper—when you celebrate wedding milestones . . . such as your fiftieth anniversary!).

TAKING INVENTORY OF YOUR VITAL STATISTICS

In the privacy of your bedroom or bathroom, you must face the brutal truth. Strip down to your birthday suit and take these all-important measurements to use as a baseline of where you are now and where you hope to be in the months ahead.

You will need a scale, a full-length mirror, a plastic tape measure, a pencil, a flat twelve-inch ruler, a calculator, and some courage. A trusted friend or family member would also be helpful for a few of the measurements.

Forget all those excuses for why the scale isn't right. It doesn't matter if it gives a different reading from the scale in the gym or your doctor's office. What matters is that *each week* you will return to *your* scale and record the change of weight that it reports. Do not get on the scale more than once a week. Body weight fluctuates from morning to night due to changes in hydration and elimination. Your weight will also fluctuate at different times throughout your menstrual cycle. This is normal. What you need to focus on are the changes in weight *over time* that are permanent, not transient.

Body weight is not the most important, or revealing, aspect of your appearance anyway. No one else actually gets to see the number on your scale. What people notice about you is the way you carry and present yourself. It's the total package. Posture and proportions are big parts of that image, along with height and weight. You can do very little about how tall you are, but you can *look* taller and thinner with better posture and certain fashion choices. You can definitely reshape proportions through weight loss (or gain) and exercise. See chapters Three, Five, and Six for more advice on these changes.

THE WEIGH-IN

Place your scale on a flat surface—preferably not on carpet or tile. If you're using a floor-model scale with a numerical read-out, set the dial so that the arrow points directly at zero. For digital scales, be sure the battery is new and the LED panel is blank (or zero) when first turned on. If you're using a balance-beam scale, slide the top and bottom weights to zero to ensure that the bar is balanced with nothing on the scale. Now step on the scale and record exactly what you weigh in pounds and ounces. (Use the charts on page 13 and 14 to record this—and other measurements—today and again before the wedding.)

YOUR TRUE HEIGHT

Find a section of wall that rises from an uncarpeted floor and has no obstructions at the base, such as a molding or heating panel. Grab your pencil and ruler. Stand barefooted with your back against the wall and your legs together. Be sure the backs of your heels, buttocks, shoulders, and head are touching the wall.

Place the ruler on your head so one end touches the wall and the other extends over your forehead. Position the ruler so it is balanced, then gently press down on the center of the ruler on top of your head. Hold the pencil in your other hand and draw a line on the wall at the point where the ruler touches it.

Step away from the wall and, using the tape measure, measure the distance between the line you drew and the floor directly below it. Convert the measurement to inches by multiplying each foot by twelve, then add any remaining inches to that for your total.

TOP-TO-BOTTOM CIRCUMFERENCE MEASUREMENTS

Take all of the following measurements while naked. We realize that one or more of these "parts" may not show when you're wearing your wedding dress—but they will on your honeymoon!

Bust: Grab one end of the flexible plastic tape measure and wrap it around your back before grabbing the other end in your free hand. Stand sideways and look into the mirror while pulling the tape up toward your armpits. Stop at the point on your back opposite the natural protrusion of your breasts.

Gently pull the end of the tape over your nipples and take a reading of the inches around your bustline.

Waist: Drop the tape down to below your ribs and above your hips where your body indents the most. Don't inhale or deliberately flatten your stomach. Exhale and take a reading of the inches around your waistline.

Hips: Looking sideways into the mirror, lower the tape so it rides over the most protruding part of your behind. Wrap the tape around, without tugging on it, so it encircles you without rising up in the front. Take a reading of the inches around your hips.

Thigh (get help, if available, for this measurement): Stand with your feet shoulder-width apart and your weight evenly distributed over each foot. Bending slightly at the waist, wrap the tape around your right leg at the thickest, uppermost part and take a reading. Now measure the left thigh. Be sure you do not bend your knees or tighten the muscles in your leg while measuring the thighs.

Calf (get help, if available, for this measurement): Stand with your weight evenly distributed on both feet and shoulder-width apart. Measure the distance between your ankle bone on the side of your foot and the crease in back of your knee.

Find the midpoint between these two spots and wrap the tape around your calf for a measurement.

Upper Arm (get help, if available, for this measurement): Raise one arm at a time directly in front of you, with palm facing up, until your extended arm is level with your shoulder. Measure the distance between the crease in your elbow and your shoulder bone. Find the midpoint between these two spots and wrap the tape around your arm, without flexing the muscle, for a measurement.

Frame: Extend the thumb and index finger of your dominant hand as if making a gun. Place your opposite wrist into the crotch of your extended fingers, then wrap your thumb and index finger around your wrist to the point at which they meet. Be sure you use only your thumb and index finger to encircle your wrist. If your thumb and index finger *overlap,* you have a small frame. If they *just meet,* you have a medium frame. If they *don't touch,* you have a large frame. Frame size is largely determined by the size and configuration of your bones, so it's not going to change if you lose weight. However, it's important to know your frame size because height-weight charts are often further categorized by frame size. In other words, if you're five feet eight with a large frame, your "healthy weight" range will be higher than that of a woman who is the same height but who possesses a smaller frame.

SURREAL VERSUS IDEAL WEIGHT

There is no law against dreaming, but let's face it: You have only a few months until the wedding. At best you can expect to lose two to three pounds a week. More likely, you will average one or two pounds a week.

On the following pages, we've included two different methods for helping you determine a *healthy* weight for your size; and the definition of "healthy" here is what places you at lowest risk of developing and/or succumbing to underweight conditions, such as osteoporosis and amenorrhea (loss of menstrual periods), and those most common in the obese—diabetes and high blood pressure. First, you'll find a weight-for-height chart—further categorized by frame size—from Metropolitan Life, an insurance company. These are good, general guidelines. The chief criticism against charts of this type, however, is that the data comes from people who are buying life insurance, not from a random population. In other words, such charts don't take into account socioeconomic or ethnic differences among people, and such differences *can* make a difference when it comes to so-called "ideal weights." For example, a typical African-American tends to have a heavier skeletal frame—which in itself does not put him or her at any additional risk of succumbing to obesity-related conditions—than a typical Caucasian. This means that an African-American's weight may be heavier—but still as

TABLE 1

Metropolitan Life Weight*-for-Height Table for Women
These ranges are for women ages 25 to 59 based on lowest mortality rates (that is, death!). *(Source: Society of Actuaries and Association of Life Insurance Medical Directors of America)*

Height		Small Frame	Medium Frame	Large Frame
Feet	Inches			
4	9	99–108	106–118	115–127
4	10	100–110	108–120	117–131
4	11	101–112	110–123	119–134
5	0	103–115	112–126	122–137
5	1	105–118	115–129	125–140
5	2	108–121	118–132	128–144
5	3	111–124	121–135	131–148
5	4	114–127	124–138	134–152
5	5	117–130	127–141	137–156
5	6	120–133	130–144	140–160
5	7	123–136	133–147	143–164
5	8	126–139	136–150	146–167
5	9	129–142	139–153	149–170
5	10	132–145	142–156	152–173
5	11	135–148	145–159	155–176

*Weights have been adjusted for barefoot height measurement.

TABLE 2

Determining Body Mass Index (BMI): The Formula
Take the following steps, or consult the chart on the next pages.

Step One: Multiply your weight in pounds by 705.
Step Two: Divide the answer by your height in inches.
Step Three: Again divide that number by your height.

EXAMPLE: Weight, 140 pounds; height, 65 inches
$$140 \times 705 = 98{,}700$$
98,700 divided by 65 = 1518
1518 divided by 65 = 23, the BMI

healthy—as what's indicated in the chart. For that reason and others, doctors often don't agree on the cutoff points for "healthy" versus "unhealthy" ranges.

Our other—and the newer—guideline for helping you determine a healthy weight is the Body Mass Index, or BMI. It's now preferred by most experts, but like the weight-for-height charts, doctors don't always agree on the healthy vs. unhealthy cutoff points. For our purposes, however, keep this general guideline in mind: *A desirable BMI in women is less than 25; you're overweight if your BMI is 25 to 30; and you're obese if your BMI is above 30.*

Although the weight goals represented in these charts may not be the same as *your* desired or ideal weight, it is important to have some idea of your weight range for good health.

TABLE 3

Determining BMI by Height and Weight Measurements

Body Mass Index

Height (in.)	Body Weight (lbs.)	20	21	22	23	24	25	26	27	28	29	30
	19											
58	91	96	100	105	110	115	119	124	129	134	138	143
59	94	99	104	114	119	124	128	133	138	138	143	148
60	97	102	197	112	118	123	128	133	138	143	148	153
61	100	106	111	116	122	127	132	137	143	148	153	158
62	104	109	115	120	126	131	136	142	147	153	158	164
63	107	113	118	124	130	135	141	146	152	158	163	169
64	110	116	122	128	134	140	145	151	157	163	169	174
65	114	120	126	132	138	144	150	156	162	168	174	180
66	118	124	130	136	142	148	155	161	167	173	179	186

TABLE 3 (cont.)

Determining BMI by Height and Weight Measurements

Height (in.)	Body Weight (lbs.)	Body Mass Index											
	19	20	21	22	23	24	25	26	27	28	29	30
67	121	127	134	140	146	153	159	166	172	178	185	191
68	125	131	138	144	151	158	164	171	177	184	190	197
69	128	135	142	149	155	162	169	176	182	189	196	203
70	132	139	146	153	160	167	174	181	188	195	202	207
71	136	143	150	157	165	172	179	186	193	200	208	215
72	140	147	154	162	169	177	184	191	199	206	213	221
73	144	151	159	166	174	182	189	197	204	212	219	227

R E C O R D   Y O U R   M E A S U R E M E N T S

List your current measurements in the column on the left; save the column on the right for recording your measurements at a date closer to your wedding, so that you can see your progress.

Date: _____   Date: _____

Weight: _____   Weight: _____

Height: _____   Height: _____

Bust: _____   Bust: _____

Waist: _____   Waist: _____

Hips: _____   Hips: _____

Thigh: Left ____ Right ____   Thigh: Left ____ Right ___

Calf: Left ____ Right ____   Calf: Left ____ Right ___

Upper Arm: Left ___ Right ___ Upper Arm: Left ___ Right ___

Frame (circle): Small/Med./Large   Frame: Small/Med./Large

BMI: _____   BMI: _____

Off-the-Rack Apparel Sizes:

Date: _____   Date: _____

Hat: _____   Hat: _____

Blouse: _____   Blouse: _____

Jacket: _____   Jacket: _____

Skirt: _____   Skirt: _____

Dress: _____   Dress: _____

Slacks: _____   Slacks: _____

Jeans: _____   Jeans: _____

Coat: _____   Coat: _____

Swimsuit: _____   Swimsuit: _____

Leotard: _____   Leotard: _____

Bra: _____   Bra: _____

Underpants: _____   Underpants: _____

Pantyhose: _____   Pantyhose: _____

Ring: _____   Ring: _____

Glove: _____   Glove: _____

Shoe: _____   Shoe: _____

CHAPTER TWO

HIDE AND SEEK . . . YOUR BEST AND WORST FEATURES

*L*ife isn't like fairy tales. When the Evil Queen in *Snow White* looked into the mirror and asked, "Who's the fairest of them all?" she was told just what she wanted to hear. And as we all know, that bit of misinformation didn't help her self-improvement program one bit!

REFLECTIONS

If you live in the real world, you need to take a long, hard look into a full-length mirror and face the bare facts reflected back at you. While many aspects of your figure and your overall appearance can be changed through diet and exercise, some things cannot, no matter how hard you try. Height is one example; the shape and bone structure of your face is another.

There is hope for your unalterable features, though, and we don't mean surgery. Styling changes—in dress, in hairstyle, in makeup—have been used by actors for centuries to create illusions. Just take a close look at entertainer Ru Paul, the grand master (madam?) of deception! If men can make up to look like glamorous women, women can do it even better.

Complete the Mirror, Mirror chart on page 18 to establish realistic goals for yourself. You will feel much more satisfied if you focus on things you can change, and see some results for your efforts, as opposed to going after the impossible and constantly feeling frustrated (which can, among other things, lead to overeating).

To get started on your diet and exercise changes, you must also take a realistic look at a calendar and your daily appointment book. How many weeks do you have till the wedding? And how many hours per week can you dedicate to serious exercise? You will need these numbers to complete the Wedding Dress Diet Worksheet in Chapter Four.

Styling changes may not take months to accomplish, but you should allow plenty of time to phase them into your life and look. Remember: This is not your high school prom. The groom shouldn't do a doubletake when you reach his side because you have changed your appearance so dramatically he doesn't recognize you. Beautiful is good, shocking is not.

Talk to a good hairstylist about color, cut, and style possibilities, keeping in mind your headpiece. Start growing out your layered look or begin trimming those long tresses so you have time to settle into your new 'do. Many hairstylists say that a haircut looks best a week after you get it, so keep that in mind when you set your prewedding appointment.

This is a good time to start thinking about your eyebrows, too. Does the color of your brows match your hair? Will you be tweezing them into thin arcs or going for a more natural look?

It's a good idea to ask your hairstylist to give you a trial run a month before your wedding. Jog around the block with the new style; that'll be no more taxing than the workout you'll put it through on the day of your wedding and reception. We know one bride who not only put her hairstylist through a trial run, but her makeup artist, too. (Her concern about the makeup artist is understandable when you know that she hired the woman who had done the makeup for the "dead" people floating in the water in the movie *Titanic*! By the way, the makeup of this thoroughly alive bride looked fabulous on her wedding day.)

If you'll be doing your own makeup, go to cosmetic counters in department stores for free advice on skin care and makeup application. You may even be able to get a free

MIRROR, MIRROR ON THE WALL

Features Changeable with Diet and Exercise

	Satisfied	Unsatisfied	Fantasy Goal	Realistic Goal
Weight				
Bust*				
Waist				
Hips*				
Stomach				
Thighs				
Calves				
Upper arms				
Neck				
Posture				

Features Improved with Styling

	Satisfied	Unsatisfied	Fantasy Goal	Realistic Goal
Hair color				
Hair length				
Eyebrows				
Complexion				
Face shape				
Facial features				
Torso length				
Bust*				
Shoulder width				
Hips*				
Leg length				

Unchangeable Features

Height	
Frame	
H-O-A-X shape (see Chapter Three)	
Shoe size	

* Some reduction and reshaping of the bust and trimming of the hips are possible, but don't expect major renovations in these areas. Use the style pointers in Chapter Three to further minimize or accentuate these features.

makeover at some concessions. Again, give yourself plenty of time to get used to applying your makeup to highlight your bone structure while masking dark circles and other liabilities. See Chapter Three for tips.

You should also read Chapter Three before you even think about shopping for your wedding dress. Take this book with you into the bridal salons to ensure that you select the most flattering gown for your figure. It is tempting, the minute you get engaged, to start flipping through the pages of bridal magazines and window shopping for a dress. But this can be dangerous! You risk falling madly in love with the wrong gown, which is almost as bad as falling for the wrong guy. Unless you're committed to wearing an heirloom dress that has been in your family for years, do not look at a wedding dress until you know exactly what you need to flatter your figure.

A V O W T O L O S E

Most people greatly underestimate how really difficult it is to lose five pounds. When you have even more than that to lose, it can be one of the toughest jobs you'll ever tackle. But it is doable. What it takes is unwavering focus and unyielding commitment—not willpower. What's the difference? Willpower is a short-lived emotion, such as being in love with capri pants while they're in fashion, then losing interest once they fade into fashion history. It dissipates with time. Commitment is a cerebral activity, something you work at and focus on because it's important to you, like learning the stats for all the players on your fiancé's favorite baseball team.

All of the good intentions in the world and wishes made on shooting stars have never made anyone thinner. When you are up against lifelong eating habits and the mindless comfort of doing things that are familiar, it is not enough to be sincere about losing weight. You must treat it as a serious business.

The first thing you have to do is to complete the Wedding Dress Diet Weight Loss Contract on page 26. Once you decide how much weight you can safely lose between today and the wedding (see the Wedding Dress Diet Worksheet in Chapter Four), you need to enlist the help of some significant supporters. You can ask your fiancé, your bridesmaids, your mom, your personal trainer, or the whole bunch of them if it will help! Each person must be informed of your weight-loss plan and given a specific role to play to help you reach your goal. They, in turn, must be willing to execute their end of the deal by providing the contracted support *and* enforcing the stated rewards and penalties.

You can use your supporters to do all kinds of things, such as shopping for food for you, cooking a meal for you, washing your gym clothes, or refusing to go to happy hour with you. A supporter's most important job is witnessing and recording your weigh-ins. As humbling an experience as this may be, it is also one of the most powerful motivators around. Do yourself a kind favor, however, by scheduling your weigh-ins for *Fridays*, not Mondays. People tend to eat more sensibly and exercise more regularly during the weekdays rather than on weekends. A Monday weigh-in can be very discouraging.

Chart your weekly weight on the Wedding Dress Diet Weight Record you'll find in this chapter. We've included both a blank chart for your use and a filled-in sample so that you can see how it works. We've set the chart up for twenty-six weeks' worth of weight recording. If you have more time than that, be sure to photocopy the blank chart before you begin filling it in.

If you reach your weekly (or monthly) weight-loss goals, you deserve to be rewarded. If you fail to reach them, you must accept a penalty—on top of the extra pounds! The rewards and penalties should be meaningful ones to you or they won't motivate you to do what you must while discouraging you from what you must not.

Money is a major source of motivation for most people. You can set up a system where you put a significant amount of cash into a kitty at the start of your program—let's say ten dollars per pound you want to lose. Each week or month that you lose the weight you need to, you can take some of that money back, at a rate of ten dollars per pound. When you don't lose, that same amount of money must be given to some-one completely undeserving, such as a lazy teenage sibling or an insufferable coworker who never repays his debts.

You may also arrange for your rewards to be in the form of favors from your supporters. Get a pampered pedicure or a bedtime backrub for a job well done. Likewise, the penalty for not losing may be that you have to clean your girlfriend's apartment or wash your fiancé's car. Whatever you decide, it has to be meaningful and enforceable to keep you on track. No lame excuses accepted.

After everyone has signed the contract, don't just stuff it into a desk drawer. Keep it out as a visible reminder of the goals you have set for yourself and the hard work that must be done to achieve them. It is very helpful to reread your con-tract once a day to refocus your attention on your goal and strengthen your resolve to see it through to the end.

When you occasionally get off track, or completely lose your way, reach out to your supporters for encouragement. Pick up the phone and call a buddy as soon as you feel your-self slipping. Ask her to read the contract aloud to you. Or solicit your signers by e-mail to send you some positive affir-mations that you *can* do it and are going to make it to the wed-ding in the size of your dreams.

Remember, losing weight is hard. If it were easy, everybody would be thin! Deciding to eat a piece of fruit every after-noon, for example, instead of a vending machine snack sounds simple enough. But to break the old habit, you must put into place several new behaviors.

First, you must have a steady supply of fresh fruit on hand, which means making regular trips to the produce market. Then you must remember to throw a piece into your bag each morning before you head off to work or to do errands. And then, when you are tired, bored, and/or frustrated in the late afternoon, you must resist the temptation to munch on something chocolatey or salty from the vending machine in the break room—a path you've walked every day at three P.M. for months—and reach into your bag for that piece of fruit.

This is the challenge, but you are as ready now as you will ever be to conquer it. You've got the ring on your finger, the date on the calendar, and the dress of your dreams to keep you going. Good luck, and may the best bride lose!

FOR BETTER AND FOR WORSE

Before you change the way you eat, you must first change the way you think. Too often, women begin weight-loss programs when they feel their very worst about themselves. Unfortunately, it only makes the job of losing weight harder if you start off believing you are a hopeless mess.

Try to imagine lending a helping hand to someone you really don't like. Are you going to go out of your way to make sure

Chewing the Fat Online

You're dying for a Ding Dong. And you've just discovered that your roommate stashed a warehouse-store-size box of them in the vegetable bin of the refrigerator. Slam the door and head for your computer. While the Internet is littered with weight-loss junk—mostly pitches for particular products—there are places to go if all you want is support. One option: "buddy boards"—electronic bulletin boards where dieters can find others who want to exchange e-mail encouragement. "Having someone I can share advice, confessions, and motivation with has made all the difference," a woman whose online name is Soonslim told <u>Cosmo</u>. If you're on America Online, find a cyberbuddy in the Thrive@Shape area.

If you're not on AOL, there are still plenty of online support sites. Author Pam Dixon, who has written five Internet guides and has also lost considerable weight herself, recommends the following:

Usenet News Groups
:alt.support.diet

Says Dixon: "The messages are very supportive. You can learn a lot from other people's experiences.

"Mostly messaging with a couple of chats. Gail Graham created the page because she couldn't find support elsewhere on the Web. One of the many features on this site is the Diet Crisis

Center, where you can leave urgent messages and get immediate support."

Diettalk
http://www.diettalk.com

"You'll find recipes and success stories here, but this is mainly a well-organized live chat page with lots of good information from experts like nutritionists, nurses, and authors."

Overeaters Recovery Group Home Page
http://www.hiwaay.net/recovery

"Many participants on this page are members of Overeaters Anonymous, but you don't have to be a member to participate, and the page has no official affiliation with OA. Most popular and famous (an Internet legend!): the Rosanne loop, a giant support group on compulsive overeating. It's been around forever."

Shape Up America's Support Center
http://www.shapeup.org

This is one we found ourselves. Shape Up America is a program instituted by ex–Surgeon General C. Everett Koop. Part of this excellent site on healthy eating and exercise is a support line, where Website visitors can post or respond to a request for support.

The Wedding Dress Diet Weight Loss Contract

I, _____, have set the following specific and measurable weight loss goal for myself. I pledge to lose _____ pounds by _____. I will follow the dietary guidelines and perform the exercise outlined in the Wedding Dress Diet Worksheet (Chapter Four) necessary to lose _____ pounds per week/month beginning on _____. It is important to me because_____.

I have made the following people aware of my goal and they have agreed to help me achieve it by doing the following things:

Support Person	**Method of Help**
#1 _____	_____
#2 _____	_____
#3 _____	_____

I will keep track of my progress by being weighed weekly/monthly. Support person # ___ will witness and enter the results of each weigh-in in the Wedding Dress Diet Weight Record. Support person # ___ will serve as the alternate for weigh-ins if the first appointee is unavailable. My reward(s) for losing the required weight at each weigh-in will be

_____.

My penalty(ies) for not losing the required weight will be _____. A signed and dated copy of this contract has been given to all those named in it.

_____ bride-to-be's signature _____ date

_____ Support person #1 _____ date

_____ Support person #2 _____ date

_____ Support person #3 _____ date

she has what she wants? Will you put her needs before your own? Is it likely you'll make personal sacrifices to see that she is happy? Probably not.

Yet if you begin a weight-loss and fitness program harboring terrible, negative feelings about yourself, it's the same thing. *You* are going to need unconditional love and plenty of nurturing to get through the rough times. It isn't possible to provide that if you think yourself unworthy of special care and attention.

Robyn will never forget a former client who really struggled to get her weight down. She rose early each morning to exercise before work and kept track of every morsel she put into her mouth. It seemed no matter how "good" she was, however, she couldn't make that scale budge more than a few ounces a week. But she didn't become discouraged. She never saw herself as a failure at weight loss. Instead, she recognized that she was doing the best she could, and she accepted the results she got. And she was able to do this because she had many other accomplishments she took pride in.

One summer she decided to refinish her basement to make a playroom for her kids. She got some estimates for the job and quickly realized it would be too expensive to hire a builder, so she decided to do it herself! She watched the home improvement shows on television and read some books on carpentry. Then she measured and designed the room and went to the building supply store for the materials. By the end of the summer, she had a cozy new playroom.

That playroom said more about her than those stubborn little pounds on her hips. She was able to accept the slow pace of her weight loss because she saw herself as more than just a number on the scale. She also realized that she could have just as easily *gained* weight over those months she was only dropping a pound or two if she hadn't held fast to her program.

What is important to remember is that having a few pounds or inches to lose does not make you a criminal. In fact, it doesn't even make you a petty offender. Your moral character cannot be judged by your body weight at all. Focusing all of your attention on a single trait, such as twenty extra pounds, can really undermine your self-confidence, which will, in turn, sabotage your efforts to lose that weight.

It is time to look at *all of* your attributes so you can see those ten, twenty, thirty, or fifty extra pounds as a minor flaw when stacked against all your other fine qualities. Once you learn to like yourself for the person you are, it will be much easier to change the packaging you walk around in. You may even come to realize that no improvements are needed after all.

Read the list of features in the chart More Than Meets the Eye on pages 30–31. Check off all that apply to you. Don't be modest. If friends tell you that you have a great sense of humor, or coworkers marvel at your creativity, then you've got it! Use the space on the bottom of the chart to list all the personal accomplishments you are most proud of, such as paying your own way through college, and your special talents, such as never forgetting anyone's birthday. Then note the things about yourself that you would never want to change.

Use this chart to keep your weight-loss goal in perspective, and to stop the flood of negative thoughts that can fill your mind when you've had a minor setback. No one is perfect. And those who think they are already have one strike against them!

More Than Meets the Eye

I am able to:

- ❑ Accept criticism
- ❑ Concentrate
- ❑ Control my temper
- ❑ Express my fears
- ❑ Show sympathy
- ❑ Make decisions
- ❑ Meet people
- ❑ _____

- ❑ Take responsibility
- ❑ Organize things
- ❑ Complete projects
- ❑ Make friends
- ❑ Have fun
- ❑ Listen
- ❑ Forgive
- ❑ _____

I have (a) good:

- ❑ Education
- ❑ Imagination
- ❑ Sense of direction
- ❑ Sense of humor
- ❑ Sense of rhythm
- ❑ Sense of style
- ❑ _____

- ❑ Reputation
- ❑ Memory
- ❑ Personality
- ❑ Religious faith
- ❑ Vocabulary
- ❑ Willpower
- ❑ _____

I am:

- ❑ Articulate
- ❑ Artistic
- ❑ Assertive
- ❑ Athletic

- ❑ Intelligent
- ❑ Loyal
- ❑ Patient
- ❑ Self-confident

❏ Creative   ❏ Self-disciplined

❏ Dependable   ❏ Self-sufficient

❏ Generous   ❏ Sensitive

❏ Graceful   ❏ Sentimental

❏ Happy   ❏ Sexy

❏ Hard-working   ❏ Thrifty

❏ Independent   ❏ Tolerant

❏ _____   ❏ _____

Accomplishments in my life I am most proud of:

Talents and/or abilities I possess that others admire in me:

Things about myself I would never want to change:

The Wedding Dress Diet Weight Record

Starting Weight: _____   Starting Date: _____

Weight Goal: _____   Goal Date: _____

WEEKS

Weigh-In Dates	1	2	3	4	5	6	7	8	9	10	11	12	13

Weigh-In Weights POUNDS

The Wedding Dress Diet Weight Record

Starting Weight: _____   Starting Date: _____

Weight Goal: _____   Goal Date: _____

WEEKS

	14	15	16	17	18	19	20	21	22	23	24	25	26
Weigh-In Dates													

Weigh-In Weights POUNDS

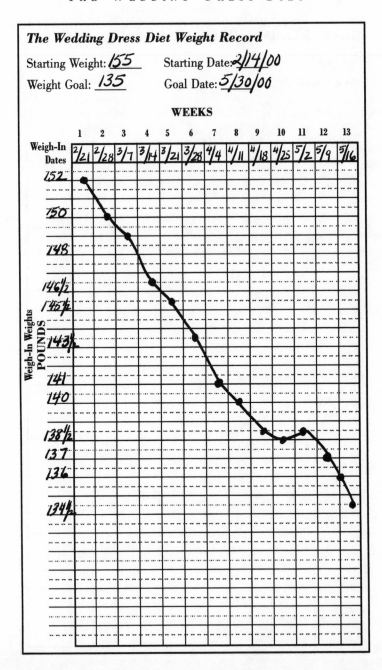

The Wedding Dress Diet Weight Record

Starting Weight: *155*   Starting Date: *2/14/00*

Weight Goal: *135*   Goal Date: *5/30/00*

The Wedding Dress Diet Weight Record

Starting Weight: **155**   Starting Date: **2/14/00**

Weight Goal: **135**   Goal Date: **5/30/00**

WEEKS

	14	15	16	17	18	19	20	21	22	23	24	25	26
Weigh-In Dates	5/23	5/30											
134													
133													

Weigh-In Weights POUNDS

CHAPTER THREE

FINDING THE PERFECT
WEDDING DRESS FOR
YOUR FIGURE

*Y*es, we know that this chapter seems too prema-
ture, coming as it does before the chapters on
diet and exercise. But there's a reason: The
maker of your bridal gown will need, at the bare minimum,
three months to make and ship your gown to the store. For
some elaborate gowns, you may have to order up to *nine
months* in advance. Most commonly, the "lead time" required
is about four to six months.

You can understand the problem with this if you haven't
yet begun the Wedding Dress Diet and your wedding is, say,

four months away. You're apt to be several pounds lighter on the day of your last fitting than you were on the day you ordered the dress. This is why it's important that you also build in at least two weeks for alterations. And take solace from this: It's much easier to take a seam *in* than to take one out.

IN PERPETUITY

The Greek philosopher Heraclitus once said, "There is nothing permanent except change." We beg to differ with his eminence. Your basic body structure is permanent, as well. We'll forgive Heraclitus, however, because he made his statement around 500 B.C. and women back then were no doubt far more preoccupied with simply surviving each day than they were with figuring out whether they were apple- or pear-shaped. The fact is, though, that even if you reach your goal weight on the Wedding Dress Diet, your basic body structure will remain the same. In other words, if your hip measurement is significantly larger than your bust size, you'll still be a pear . . . albeit a *thin* pear. And you'll still look better in some styles than you will in those designed to complement your opposite type: the woman who is bigger on top than on the bottom.

We think "pear or apple?" is far too broad a generalization, however. We much prefer the "H-O-A-X" system of body type classification. Not long ago, Jacqueline had the pleasure of interviewing the woman who developed the H-O-A-X system, Mary Duffy, long employed by the Ford Model Agency in New York City as something of a new-model mentor. Basically, each letter—H, O, A, and X—visually represents a body type. An "X" structure, for example, describes a woman with an hourglass figure; a woman whose bust and hip measurements are almost identical, while her waist measurement is significantly smaller. (Duffy wrote a book called *The H-O-A-X Fashion Formula: Dress the Body You Have to Look Like the Body You Want.* The book is out of print, but you might find a copy in your local library.)

We're going to use the H-O-A-X system, the apple vs. pear division, plus many more specific classifications in the next several pages to help you choose a gown that will both maximize your assets and minimize those you're not so proud of. Circle all the descriptions that apply to you and make notes to take along on your shopping forays. Besides your style preferences, the bridal consultant will want to know your budget, your wedding date, and the relative formality of your ceremony.

First, however, here's a glossary of the wedding apparel terms we'll be using. Keep in mind that these aren't the *only* styles you'll run into in the bridal shop; they're just the ones we suggest in the pages to come.

GLOSSARY OF STYLE TERMS

Silhouette Styles:

A-line: Resembles the letter A in that it hugs the body at the shoulders and then flares gradually away from the bodice to the hem. It doesn't have a distinct waistline.

Ballgown: Often paired with a fitted bodice, this gown has a full skirt.

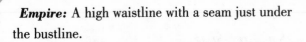

Empire: A high waistline with a seam just under the bustline.

Princess: Snug fitting on the top, it has a seamless (nondistinct) waistline, then flares slightly to the hem.

Sheath: A straight and usually long dress that hugs the body.

Necklines:

Band: This neckline has a collar that encircles the neck, something like a mock turtleneck.

Jewel: Circles the natural neckline.

Keyhole yoke: Generally, a high-necked dress with cutouts at the throat and/or bustline.

Portrait: Off the shoulders.

V-neck: This angled neckline forms a V shape.

Waistlines:

Basque: An elongated waist that drops to a point, or V, in the center of the front of the dress.

Dropped: The waistline seam is a number of inches below the natural waist.

Empire: A high waistline with a seam just under the bustline.

Natural: The waist seam is placed at the narrowest part of the midriff.

Skirts:

Apron: Extra material that falls from the waist much like a kitchen apron. Gives the skirt a fuller look.

Bustle: A gathering of fabric on the outside back of the skirt—sometimes enhanced with no-show padding—to puff out the skirt and make for a "perkier" bottom.

Flounced or tiered: A skirt with many layers.

Peplum: A flounce or short, flared flap attached at the waist of the dress and puffing out at the hips to enhance—or create—an hourglass figure.

Sleeves:

Cap sleeves: Just barely cover the shoulders; short and fitted.

Headpieces:

Juliet: This small hat hugs the back of the head.

Pillbox: Made famous by Jackie Onassis in the 1960s, this is a round, brimless hat that sits on top of the head.

Tiara: A crown resplendent with pearls, rhinestones, crystals, or other dazzling gems (faux or not).

Veils:

Ballet or waltz length: Reaches to the ankles or floor.

MAXIMIZE/MINIMIZE WITH YOUR DRESS AND ACCESSORIES

Circle all the assets/liabilities that apply. Take notes and *then* go shopping.

"I have a small waist": Emphasize it with a fitted bodice and a natural or princess waistline.

"My waist is too thick": Team a higher-waisted bodice (such as an empire style) with an A-line skirt.

I'm short-waisted": Balance yourself with a basque, dropped, or other low waistline (except if you're short in height, as well).

"I'm a little buxom": Show off your voluptuousness with a strapless gown, or one with a portrait or deep V neckline or a keyhole yoke.

"I'm too buxom": You want to draw the eye *down*. Do so with an elongated bodice (such as basque style) and a full skirt. Treat empire-waisted dresses like the plague; styles that are pinched in at the natural waistline will also emphasize your voluptuousness. Avoid froufrou on the bodice, a low neckline, and puffy sleeves. Go for lace or detailing on the skirt's hemline.

"I have a long, graceful neck": Keep your eye out for dresses with a band neckline or a high-necked keyhole yoke.

"My neck is too skinny": Necklaces and chokers are great disguises.

"I have long, shapely legs": Search for a short dress or a long sheath that's split to the thigh. Soap opera star Liz Keifer won raves from *People* magazine for her "casually elegant" above-the-knee wedding dress and coat ensemble by Isaac Mizrahi. "Her outfit looks terrific for a daytime wedding," designer John Scher told *People*. "She could even wear this afterward."

"My legs are heavy": If you're wearing a short dress—though a long dress might be better for you—opt for sheer or opaque stockings. Avoid stockings with heavy textures. Avoid shoes with ankle straps. Look for a chunky heel; skinny heels

on your shoes will also call attention to the heaviness of your legs.

"My legs are too skinny": If you're wearing a short dress, you're the person who can benefit from heavy-textured stockings. If your dress reveals your legs, make sure it's not so full as to make your legs look like straws.

"I have shapely arms": Sleeveless dresses, those with cap sleeves, and those with portrait necklines are all good choices.

"My arms are too plump": Opt for long, thin—but not skintight—sleeves.

"My arms are too skinny": Again, go for long sleeves that are not skintight. If you fall in love with a shorter-sleeved dress, consider camouflaging your arms with upper-arm bracelets.

"I have gorgeous hands and nails": Attract the eye to them with long sleeves that taper to a point on the back of your hand.

"I have bony shoulders/protruding collarbone": Detract from them with a high neckline. Avoid clingy fabrics (such as

jersey) and big puffed sleeves; the latter will make you look like you're drowning!

"*I have broad shoulders*": "Narrow" them with a draped, wide-collared or V neckline. Avoid shoulder pads and puffed sleeves, as well as halter dresses and deeply scooped necklines.

"*I have small hips*": You can beautifully pull off wearing a gown with a bustle, peplum, and/or apron.

"*I am tall and slim*": Choose a ballgown-type wedding dress or a long, narrow sheath.

"*I'm too tall and too thin*": A dropped waist will balance you out. Indulge yourself: You can wear as many ruffles as your heart desires. Big, puffy sleeves will also look terrific. Avoid skintight or clingy fabrics.

"*I'm too thin*" (*whatever your height*): Low necklines and skirts that are tiered or flounced will make you look fuller. Avoid skintight or clingy fabrics.

"*I'm short and chubby*": Opt for a high waistline—such as the empire—a blousy bodice, and long, narrow (but not skintight) sleeves. Choose a gathered waist (especially the basque) to make you appear taller. Stay away from puffy and/or flounced skirts. Choose a Juliet cap for your headpiece.

"I'm short—average or thin—and want to look taller": A high waistline (like the empire) will give the illusion of more height, but so, on the other hand, will the deep V of a basque waistline. Avoid full skirts and full trains . . . a chapel-length train is right for you. So is a ballet- or waltz-length veil that skims the body rather than billowing around it. Other ways to add "height": Choose a high neckline and short, straight sleeves or, if your arms are good, go sleeveless with long gloves. If you choose a short dress, wear pumps rather than shoes with ankle straps, which tend to make you look shorter by cutting off your feet at the ankle. Buy stockings similar if not identical in color to your dress; this will give the impression of a longer line. Your headpiece of choice: the Juliet cap.

"I'm overweight" ***(no matter what your height)***: Be on the lookout for gowns with vertical lines, such as those provided by high-neckline styles that just skim the body (the princess cut or an empire waist with an A-line skirt). Another way to create vertical lines is to wear a long strand of pearls or beads. No puffed sleeves! And don't buy a dress in a clingy or thick (such as velvet) fabric. When you go to choose a headpiece, lean toward a Juliet cap.

"*My feet are too big*": Opt for a pump with a squared-off or rounded toe or go with an open-toe shoe. Shoes with pointed toes—especially those with sling backs—make feet look even longer than they are.

"*I have a round, full face*": You can add height with a tiara or pillbox hat. For your dress, opt for vertical lines—long strands of beads or pearls can help here. Choose a V-neck over a rounded, scoop neckline.

"*I have a long, narrow face*": If you're hoping to achieve a serene, old-fashioned look, add width with a wide-brimmed hat. Otherwise, you can add width to your face by wearing a light-colored headband or a tiara that is low and broad.

"*I wear glasses*": A tiara will be especially flattering.

H - O - A - X   H I N T S

These are drawn from Mary Duffy's H-O-A-X system of classifying body types. See the beginning of this chapter for more information.

"*H*": This is the ladderlike figure; one that's straight up and down with no curves. Create curves by selecting a style that emphasizes both your bustline and your hips, preferably one that's equal in both areas. What will help: oversize shoulders, a jewel neckline, a cinched, natural waistline, and a full, billowing skirt. Avoid narrow sheaths and empire and other high-waisted styles. They'll add to your "H-ness."

"O": The woman with this figure type tends to look round; she carries most of her excess weight in her midriff area. This kind of body is also often accompanied by relatively slender legs—so play them up with a short dress or a longer one that's slit up the side. Give yourself a more "hourglass" appearance by looking for a dress that has an indented (but not fitted) waist and a blousy-style bodice. A V neckline is also a good choice for you.

"A": The pear-shaped figure. Shoot for styles that are narrow above the waist and wide below. A princess-line gown will narrow your shape while still showing off your feminine curves. Opt for full sleeves that make your shoulders look broader; a high neckline is a no-no because it will make your shoulders look narrower, emphasizing your pear-like silhouette. Also avoid narrow, sheathlike styles.

"X": The hourglass body type. You meet the qualifications if your bust and hip measurements are the same and your waist is about ten inches smaller. Choose a ballgown look—low neckline, off-the-shoulder sleeves, a narrow waistline, and a full skirt. Take a pass on high-waisted styles—they hide all of your assets!

MAKEUP THAT MAXIMIZES/ MINIMIZES

Here's the basic principle: Light maximizes, dark minimizes. Use highlights (the "light") and contours (the "dark") to play up or play down your features. You can purchase products especially designed for highlighting or contouring. Or, for highlighting, use a slightly lighter shade of foundation than the one you wear on the rest of your face; lighter-toned cover stick, cream, or liquid; or translucent or pearlized powder. For contouring, you can also try a foundation in a slightly darker shade than you wear on the rest of your face or a gel or powder blush. The following tips are for that "extra-special" look you'll want on your wedding day; they're probably a bit "too too" for everyday wear.

"My face is too round": Contour with inverted triangles of blush that start on your cheekbones, stretch under the outer two-thirds of your eyes, and that are well-blended up and out toward your ears and the outer corners of your eyes. Do keep in mind that a bottom-heavy or round face never kept

Andie MacDowell or Minnie Driver from getting plum movie roles.

"My cheeks are too fat": Concentrate your blush or other contour away from the center of your face. Sweep it on the sides of your face from the lower lip line to just about an inch or two above your eyebrow.

"My face is too long and thin": Use a contourer on the upper third of your forehead. Also, put a rectangle of blush along the tops of your cheekbones, starting at a point below the outer third of the eye and blending up and outward all the way out to the ear, then up along the hairline till it's just a tad higher than the eyebrows.

"My cheekbones are too high": Concentrate your contour (blush in this case) on the center of your face, closer to your nose.

"I have a double chin": "Firm" yourself up by applying contour under the chin (but no lower than the first extra chin) from behind the earlobe, circling around the underside of the jawbone, and crossing beneath the natural chinbone.

"My neck is too short": Apply contour (in this case, blush would probably work best) down the sides of the neck, blending well. This will give the illusion of a longer neck.

HAIRSTYLES THAT HELP

"I have a round face": Do avoid slicked-back and very short hair. A few face-framing curls are in order, as is a definite side part.

"My cheeks are too fat": Choose a style that will give you softness and height at the crown and that will keep your hair close to the head on the sides. The latter will give your cheeks the "shadows" that they're missing.

"My face is too long and thin": You want fullness and softness on the sides of your head. Straight bangs will help, as well.

"My neck is too fat": Opt for a style that's short and simple and keep your hair clear of your neckline.

KNOW BEFORE YOU GO (SHOPPING)

- *Look behind you.* Pay attention to the way the dress looks from behind. That's the way guests will be seeing you at least half of the time.
- *No Nordstrom's, they.* Most bridal shops will require a deposit when you place your order. Oftentimes, if you can-

cel, you'll not only forfeit that deposit, you'll have to pay for the rest of the dress, as well. Before placing your order, ask about the shop's cancellation policy.

- *Welcome to your new, bigger size.* Most wedding dresses run small, at least a size or two, and you'll find this to be especially true if you're busty or broad-shouldered. At any rate, don't faint at the bridal consultant's announcement that you need, say, a size fourteen instead of your regular size ten.

- *But you'll probably feel pretty small in another way* . . . and that's in terms of length. Most gowns are made to fit a woman who is five foot eight. Hemming may be on your horizon.

- *Dress to impress.* When you go for fittings, wear undergarments and accessories that are similar or the same as the ones you plan to wear on your wedding day, such as a push-up Wonderbra, shapewear, light stockings, and high heels.

- *Home shopping.* Besides studying the bridal magazines, you can get lots of ideas from the hundreds of Websites devoted to wedding dresses. Just type in the key words *wedding dresses* or *wedding gowns* where your search engines ask for them. One Website we particularly like is Wedding Channel.com. There's a page on this Website that will show you gowns based on your preferences in silhouette, waistline, length, neckline, sleeve length, sleeve style, fabric type, skirt style, train style, and color.

Tragic. But True.

For a break from the stress of finding that perfect dress, don't miss a Website that features a page called "What Were They Thinking?" (Address: http://www.visi.com/~dheaton/bride/what_were_they_thinking.html) You'll find pictures of strange, odd, and unflattering wedding dresses and accessories . . . with hilarious captions. Example: "Run! Run! It landed on your butt!" The woman depicted is wearing a way-too-big bustle. Enjoy!

PICTURE PERFECT

Of course you'll want to show off your new look—and your new dress—to best advantage in your wedding photos. We got the following tips from professional photographer Stephen Trobaugh, who has shot dozens of weddings in southern California.

While standing for a photo: Place your feet slightly apart in a modified T position—that is, with your "leading" foot pointing straight at the camera and the other foot behind it and nearly perpendicular to the heel of the lead foot. Put your weight on the back foot and slightly bend your front knee. Put your shoulders back and turn the upper part of your body toward the camera. This position is halfway between a profile and a straight-on shot and makes for the best silhouette. A straight-on shot would emphasize any "hippiness"; a profile would do the same for a problem tummy or butt.

If you're not holding flowers, lightly rest your leading hand on your thigh. Your other arm can be slightly behind your back or down the side of the corresponding thigh.

When sitting: Again, your body should not be faced directly at the camera. Sit on the *edge* of the chair (slight camera lens distortion is exaggerated when you lean away from the camera; it can make you look "slouchy"). Sit up straight, knees together, one foot in front of the other. For a graceful look, clasp your hands and place them on top of one leg or the other—not in the middle. Same goes for flowers.

About eyeglasses: If you'll be wearing them in your pictures, you'll have to lower your chin a bit so that the camera flash won't hit the middle of your glasses, obscuring your eyes. If a slight downward tilt of your head would make for—or emphasize—a double chin, you can also prevent flash glare by sliding your glasses down your nose a bit.

If you regularly wear glasses but will not be wearing them in your photos, be sure to take them off about fifteen minutes in advance so that your red "nose marks" will have faded, or use a concealer.

About undergarments: Surprisingly, Stephen Trobaugh told us that the problem he encounters most often in wedding photography is that someone's bra strap or even the top of her bra is showing. Pin judiciously! And assign a woman who is not in the wedding party to be especially alert for this problem during every posed photograph.

Another undergarment problem Trobaugh has faced is that a bridesmaid's dress or even the bride's gown is so sheer that lingerie shows through in flash pictures. Keep that in mind when you shop for your wedding finery.

About background: Let's say you and your bridesmaids are having your prewedding pictures taken at your mom's house. Her flowered wallpaper, striped drapes, and photo-covered paneled walls have been around so long that you don't really "see" them anymore. Well, that'll change when you get your wedding photos back and those backgrounds are "busy" or they clash horribly with your bridesmaids' dresses. Try to see potential backgrounds as if you are looking through the eyes of a stranger, and opt for a setting that's color complementary or undistracting. A fireplace is a good example of the latter.

About crying: You're bound to do some crying and a lot of kissing on your big day. Before every picture, ask your maid of honor if you need to touch up your lipstick or wipe off a smudge of mascara. Put together a fix-it kit—lipstick, concealer, mascara, a mirror, and a small container of nonoily eye makeup remover and Q-Tips. Carry the kit in one of those satin bridal pouch purses you wear dangling from your wrist. One enterprising bride we know even had a pocket sewn into her wedding gown in which to keep her fix-its. This may be just the right option for you if the skirt of your dress is full.

CHAPTER FOUR

THE CALORIE COUNTDOWN

*D*iets come and diets go, but calories are forever. No matter how clever the latest weight-loss gimmick of the month might sound, it all boils down to the calories at the weigh-in.

Your Wedding Dress Diet is anchored by the number of calories you eat each day and the amount of vigorous activity you perform each week. There are several different ways to space the timing of your meals and combine the foods you eat at them. This will not affect how fast or how much weight you lose.

What kind of foods those calories come from does matter,

however, and we need to deal with this first before we talk about calorie counting. Adult humans simply don't need that much protein or fat to maintain a healthy body or to prevent disease. Excess fat in the diet can clog the arteries and increases cancer risk, even if you manage to keep your weight under control. Excess protein taxes the kidneys and depletes the bones of calcium—and that's something most women can't afford to lose. On the other hand, we need a good source of fuel twenty-four hours a day. Carbohydrates are the best possible form of fuel for humans. Ideally, you should get a small number of your daily calories from fat (such as oil, soft margarine, or butter), a moderate amount from protein (such as lean meats, poultry, and fish), and the greatest amount from carbohydrates (such as bread, cereals, fruits, and many vegetables). In percentages, this means you should get 20 percent of your total calories from fat, 25 percent from protein, and the remaining 55 percent from carbohydrates. You can use the chart below to determine the number of grams of fat, protein, and carbohydrate recommended for different calorie levels based on these percentages.

NUTRITION BASICS

The simplest and most reliable way to ensure that your diet is nutritionally sound is to eat for *color*, *texture*, and *calcium*.

Distributing Your Calories			
Calories	Fat Grams	Protein Grams	Carbohydrate Grams
1,200	27	75	165
1,300	29	80	180
1,400	31	87	193
1,500	33	94	206
1,600	35	100	220
1,700	38	106	234
1,800	40	112	248
1,900	42	119	261
2,000	44	125	275

For color, choose at least three servings of fruit each day *and* three vegetables in shades of red, orange, green, and yellow (see the chart opposite; sample serving sizes provided on page 77). The produce aisle is packed with the vitamins, minerals, and phytochemicals (cancer fighters) that will keep your hair, skin, and nails glowing and your immune system strong. You can vary your selections with the seasons and enjoy your produce fresh, frozen without sugar, canned in natural juice, dried, or as 100-percent juice to meet your quota. In the case of the latter, however, don't "drink" all of your fruits and vegetables. Yes, such juices are chockful of the same vitamins

Color Schemes for Good Health

Red	Orange	Green	Yellow
Apples	Apricots	Asparagus	Bananas
Beets	Cantaloupe	Bok choy	Casabas
Cherries	Carrots	Broccoli	Corn
Plums	Mangoes	Collard greens	Grapefruit
Raspberries	Orange juice	Grapes	Lemons
Red cabbage	Peaches	Figs	Onions
Salsa	Pumpkins	Honeydew	Papayas
Strawberries	Tangerines	Pears	Pineapples
Sweet peppers	Winter squash	Snow peas	Turnips
Tomatoes	Yams	Spinach	Wax beans

and phytochemicals as solid produce, but they don't pack the fiber . . . or the chewing satisfaction! (Be sure to thoroughly wash your fruits and vegetables before eating or cooking.)

Texture comes from chewy whole grains and cereals and the stone-ground flours and meals made from them. Because whole grains still have their outer bran layer intact, they are higher in fiber than their white, refined counterparts. Fiber fills us up without filling us out. These grains are also high in complex carbohydrates, the kind that supply a steady source of energy for hours after eating them. Look for the claim "Rich in Whole Grains" on the front of the package. It guarantees the product contains at least 51 percent whole-grain flour or cereal. Choose at least three servings a day of the following wholesome, high-fiber, high-energy foods to keep you going all day, and all night, if necessary.

The Taste of Texture

Whole Grains	Cereals	Flour/Meal Products
Brown rice	Bran flakes	Bran muffin
Barley	Granola	Corn bread
Buckwheat	Grape Nuts	Polenta
Bulgur, cracked wheat	Grits	Popcorn
Quinoa	Muesli	Ry-Krisp crackers
Rye	Oatmeal	Soba noodles
Wild rice	Puffed kashi	Tabouli
Wheat berries	Shredded wheat	Tortilla
	Wheat germ	Whole wheat pasta

Calcium is a critical nutrient for women of all ages, not just little girls. If you have been careless about your intake of calcium-rich dairy products up to now, it is time to take your bones seriously before they leave you slouching. During your childbearing years, you need at least three servings a day of high-calcium foods (300 mgs. per serving). If you can't or you won't or you don't eat at least three good sources of calcium every day (See table on page 64.), buy a supplement today and take 1,000 mgs. until your twenty-fifth wedding anniversary (or until age fifty). Then you can increase the dose to

1,500 mgs. a day for the rest of your life. You may wish to try one of two recently introduced "chewy" calcium supplements: CalBurst, (800) 276-2878 or http://www.Naturemade.com; or Viactiv, (800) 247-7893 or http://www.viactiv.com. Another recently introduced product is Nugum Calcium Chewing Gum, (800) 808-4866 or http://www.gum-tech.com.

The recommended daily servings of these basic foods will supply approximately 800 calories. You should also have at least one good source of protein. Once these nutrient requirements are met, you are free to fill in the rest of your calorie "budget" with an eating plan to match your personal schedule and food preferences. But always remember that no weight-loss program can succeed without your paying strict attention to calories in and energy out.

WORKING OUT YOUR WORKOUT

Vigorous, *aerobic* exercise is necessary to use up the calories you have stored in your body as fat. There is a difference between this type of exercise and that done to improve general fitness, such as a daily walk. You have to *work off* those pounds accumulated at past meals and snacks. This can't be done by taking a stroll in the park. In fact, we're not even talking "walk" here. Think speed walking, or jogging, or running if you want to get that weight off. These are aerobic.

Calcium-to-Calories Connection

Calcium Source	Serving Size	Calcium	Calories
Fat-free milk	8 oz.	300	85
Skim Plus milk	8 oz.	300	100
Whole milk	8 oz.	300	150
Powdered nonfat milk	1/4 cup	375	110
Lactaid fortified low-fat milk	8 oz.	500	100
Soy milk, fortified	8 oz.	300	120
Rice milk, fortified	8 oz.	300	100
Orange juice, fortified	8 oz.	350	110
Yogurt, low-fat and sweetened	8 oz.	300	250
Yogurt, low-fat, plain	8 oz.	400	130
Yogurt, frozen, fat-free with added calcium	1/2 cup	450	90
Evaporated whole milk	4 oz.	330	170
Cottage cheese, low-fat with added calcium	1/2 cup	200	80
Ricotta cheese, fat-free	1/2 cup	270	100
Cocoa, sugar-free and fortified	1 packet	300	50
Cereal bar, fortified	1 bar	200	130
American cheese	1 oz.	175	105
Soy cheese, fortified	1 oz.	200	75

Exercise Heart Rate Chart

Age	Start-up Rate	Intermediate Rate	Experienced Rate
	(55% maximum)	*(65% maximum)*	*(75% maximum)*
18	111	131	151
20	110	130	150
22	109	129	149
24	108	127	147
26	107	126	146
28	106	125	144
30	105	124	143
32	103	122	141
34	102	121	140
36	101	120	138
40	99	117	135

Aerobic exercise can be measured by your heart rate during the workout—not by how much you have perspired or how long you've been exercising. When completing your Wedding Dress Diet Worksheet (see page 70), use the chart above to find the exercise heart rate you need to achieve. An explanation of how to measure your exercise heart rate—and also how to calculate your level if you're over forty years old—can be found in Chapter Five on page 98.

Once you know what your exercise heart rate is and how to measure it, you must choose a type of exercise that raises your heart rate to your target level, and you must be able to sustain that activity for thirty minutes or more. How long and how often you work out at your exercise heart rate will determine how fast and how much weight you will ultimately lose.

Resistance exercises, such as weight lifting, are discussed in Chapter Five. They help to increase the amount of muscle in your body, which raises your metabolism and aids weight loss. Resistance exercises are also used to tone and shape the muscles and have also been shown to increase bone density.

CALCULATING YOUR CALORIC ALLOWANCE

Follow these three steps to complete the Wedding Dress Diet Worksheet on page 70.

Step #1. Use the BMI chart on page 10 to determine the high and low weight range for your height. This is generally the weight that falls between a BMI of 20 and 24. The weight range for each height allows for differences in frame size and body composition. Your weight goal should fall within this range. If it doesn't, you may be aiming too low or too high. If you are extremely muscular, you may have to accept a higher weight since muscle weighs more than fat.

Once you have established a healthy goal weight, subtract that number from your present weight. Next, count how many full weeks you have left until the wedding. A weight loss of one to two pounds a week is what you can safely and comfortably expect.

Now divide the number of pounds you want to lose by the number of weeks until the wedding. If the number is greater than two—that is, more than two pounds per week of weight loss—you will have to readjust your goal to a higher weight or accept a much stricter limit on caloric intake while increasing your energy output, as outlined in Step #3.

Step #2. Multiply your goal weight by the activity factor below that matches your time commitment to exercise. The times given are for total hours *per week* of vigorous aerobic exercise performed at your exercise heart rate. Two hours of a vigorous recreational sport, such as soccer, field hockey, or racquetball, can replace one hour of aerobic exercise.

Since all good intentions can be undermined by natural

Activity Factor Chart

Total Exercise per Week	Activity Factor
Maximum output: 6–7 hours	16
Outstanding output: 5–6 hours	14
Exemplary output: 4–5 hours	13
Acceptable output: 3–4 hours	12
Notable output: 2–3 hours	11
Better than nothing: 1–2 hours	10

disasters, procrastination, and lack of time, you need a back-up plan. Calculate at least three levels of caloric intake for yourself based on three *different* exercise goals. One can be the greatest number of hours a week you can conceivably work out, another the more realistic number of hours you're likely to work out, and the third the least number of hours a week you will ever let yourself squeak by with.

With these numbers in hand, you can adjust your daily caloric intake to match your output as the weeks pass. If you don't make the adjustment and continue to eat as if you were exercising five hours a week when, in fact, you've only gotten in three hours, you are not going to lose the weight you need to.

If you exceed your daily calorie allowance only once in a while, you can make up for the excess eating by increasing your output in that week. Every 200 extra calories you eat require another thirty minutes of exercise.

Step #3 (optional). If your calculations in Step #1 indicate you need to lose two to three pounds per week, and you don't want to settle for a higher weight goal, you must make additional adjustments to your plan. First, you must add one more hour of exercise to your weekly workouts, even if you based your calculations on the maximum range of six to seven hours per week. You must also subtract 200 calories from your daily allowance. But pay close attention to the calories-for-height restrictions below. If you hit the lowest calorie level recom-

Calories-for-Height Restrictions Chart	
Height	*Lowest Caloric Intake*
4'll"–5'1"	1,000
5'2"–5'4"	1,200
5'5"–5'7"	1,400
5'8"–5'10"	1,600

mended for your height, don't go any lower. You will only slow down your weight loss if your caloric intake is insufficient to meet your basic needs. Why frustrate yourself? Work on styling ideas instead.

KEEPING TABS ON YOURSELF

You now know the caloric "budget" you must live on to lose those unwanted pounds in time for your walk down the aisle. The next thing you need is a way to stick to that budget.

If you happen to be good at managing your checkbook, you should have no difficulty managing your caloric budget. Actually, it requires the same skills. You write down a lot of numbers, then do some simple addition and subtraction. If you're not really good at money management, this diet will certainly help you get better at it. Just think, you might actu-

The Wedding Dress Diet Worksheet

(photocopy and attach to contract prepared and signed in Chapter Two)

STEP #1

Weight range for height, _____ to _____ pounds
according to BMI: low   high

Goal weight: _____ pounds

Present weight: _____ pounds

Weight to be lost: _____ pounds

Weeks until wedding: _____ weeks

Weight loss per week
to reach goal: $\underset{\text{\# lbs. to lose}}{_____} \div \underset{\text{\# weeks}}{_____} = \underset{\text{pounds/week}}{_____}$

STEP #2

Weight Goal × Activity Factor = Calories Per Day

$_____ \times \underset{\text{greatest exercise time}}{_____} = _____$

$_____ \times \underset{\text{reasonable exercise time}}{_____} = _____$

$_____ \times \underset{\text{least exercise time}}{_____} = _____$

STEP #3 (if trying to lose 2–3 pounds per week)

$\underset{\text{initial calories}}{_____} - 200 \text{ calories} = \underset{\text{adjusted calories}}{_____}$

Planned hrs. exercise per wk. _____ + 1 additional hr. = _____

ally lose weight *and* save some money at the same time. Not a bad deal!

Here's how it works. When you go shopping or pay your bills, you must record the exact amount for each check written so you can see that your balance covers your expenses, right? When trying to lose weight, you must write down the caloric value for everything you eat to be sure you're not going over your daily caloric allowance.

Typically, this is where the groaning and moaning begins. But there is no point in complaining about record keeping. No one can accurately keep track of everything she eats without writing it down. If you were so good at keeping track of what you eat in the first place, you would be thin already!

Research has shown that the people most successful at losing weight and keeping it off are the ones who kept the best food logs. Other studies have demonstrated that when overweight people are interviewed about what they eat, they often underreport their intake by as much as 20 percent. That can add up to a lot of unreported calories.

Truth is, if you do a really good job at keeping your food records for the first two weeks, the job becomes much easier after that. You will start to remember the values for the foods you eat regularly, and can refer back to former records for items eaten only occasionally.

Some people get frustrated when they can't find an exact

calorie value for each and every morsel they eat, so they give up and stop recording anything at all. If you're one of these people, lighten up! The world isn't perfect and some things just aren't knowable. But you can make an educated guess and move on. The worst thing you can do is give yourself an excuse to eat whatever you want when you decide not to keep tabs on yourself anymore. An extra thousand calories can be downed in less time than it takes to say "Häagen-Dazs."

Figuring out the caloric (or fat or sodium) values on packaged foods is no problem since all the information you need—at least in the U.S.—can be found right on the Nutrition Facts panel. Just remember to check the serving size listed on the panel. If you eat more or less than that amount, you must adjust your nutrition calculations accordingly. Bear in mind that the serving sizes listed by some manufacturers are absurdly small.

If you don't have a food label to help you, use a calorie guide available in any bookstore or online bookseller. We recommend several good ones in Chapter Eight. These guides contain the nutrition information for foods without labels, such as fresh fruits, vegetables, and meats. They also contain the values for most brand-name packaged foods and many chain restaurant menu items. Be sure to get a guide with a current copyright date since the ingredients in commercial food products often change.

The Calorie Countdown

COUNT, MEASURE, AND WEIGH
EACH AND EVERY DAY

Once you have your own pocket calorie guide, you can figure out the values for everything you put in your mouth—and that's just what you must be willing to do. No exceptions. Every Tic Tac, broken cookie, stray french fry, and swig of his beer must be duly recorded and added to your total.

What you will quickly realize, as every veteran calorie counter before you has, is that calories are tied to quantities. You know, things like ounces of turkey, cups of pasta, and number of pretzels. This is the line that divides the losers and the gainers. If you aren't prepared to take control of how much you *really* eat, as opposed to the amount you think you ate or guess you ate or estimate you ate, you may be off by hundreds of calories a day! Without question, ladies, it is portion control that separates the size sixes from the size twelves.

Another food fact you'll no doubt pick up on is that anything high in fat is also high in calories. If you want to make those precious calories last longer, steer clear of very high-fat foods. This means anything deep fried, most breakfast meats, regular ground beef, full-fat cheeses, and, of course, those rich pastries and confections loaded with butter and shortening.

But keep in mind, too, that no food is forbidden. Whatever your taste buds demand can be put into your budget—just don't get carried away or you won't be able to squeeze into that wedding gown.

What you must be prepared to do is juggle your calories to make some of the higher-fat food choices fit. Fortunately, there are plenty of very low-fat and low-calorie fruits and vegetables to fill up on the rest of the day after you eat that high-fat, high-calorie hot dog and bag of peanuts at the baseball game.

So how will you go about mastering your portion control? You can start by buying a food scale, a set of measuring cups, and a set of measuring spoons. Then you can spend a week checking the capacity of every drinking glass, coffee mug, cereal bowl, dessert dish, wineglass, soup ladle, etc., in your household. Once you know how much each of these utensils holds, you won't have to remeasure every food and drink you consume from them. A two-cup cereal bowl will never be able to hold two and a half cups of cereal and milk.

Making careful observations of the serving sizes for foods you prepare or eat at home will also help train your eye for those occasions when you are eating out and cannot weigh and measure your food. Even then, there are ways to make accurate estimates. For some helpful guidelines, see the Relative Food Portions section on page 78.

Armed with these record-keeping tools, you are now ready to start writing. You'll find the sample Wedding Dress Diet Food and Fitness Log on pages 80 to 81. You can photocopy both the sample and blank logs to use on pages 216 to 219, or design a spreadsheet on your computer, or write the headings onto the pages of a small notebook. What you choose to use for your log is entirely up to you, as long as it is convenient for you and gets the job done.

INSTRUCTIONS FOR COMPLETING THE FOOD AND FITNESS LOG

Once you have a place to record your food and fitness activities, keep it handy and be ready to write whenever you eat. Start each day by entering the day of the week and the date on the top of a new record. Then:

1. Note the time whenever you eat or drink anything and write it on your log before listing the foods and beverages you consumed.

2. Record the amount of each item eaten or drunk using actual weight in ounces or pounds, or the volume in cups or measuring spoons, or the counted number of pieces, or the size in inches.

3. Describe the food using the brand name (such as Cheerios cereal) or type of food (chicken breast). List each item individually if you have a combination food. For example, your ham and cheese sandwich should be recorded as "2

slices rye bread, 3 ounces boiled ham, 1 ounce Swiss cheese, 1 tablespoon mustard."

4. Note any special features of the foods, such as "reduced-calorie version," or "cooked in broth in wok," or "skin removed from chicken," or "homemade recipe," or "fortified with extra calcium."

5. Look up the caloric value for each item and calculate the actual number of calories in the amount you ate. You may want to subtotal your daily calories after each meal so that you know how many more you have left to work with that day.

6. Indicate if any item is a full or partial serving of your daily requirement for fruits/vegetables, grains, or calcium-rich foods and write in the number under the appropriate heading. This will let you know how you're doing nutrition-wise. See Standardized Serving Sizes—on the opposite page and page 78—for examples of standardized portions for these foods.

7. Total your calories at the end of the day. Also total the number of servings of fruits/vegetables, grains, and calcium.

8. Enter what type of aerobic exercise you did and for how long, and whether your exercise heart rate was monitored and maintained.

9. Indicate whether you completed your scheduled resistance workout for upper and lower body and abdominal exercises.

10. Circle whether or not you have taken your required supplements.

11. Circle whether or not you achieved your food and fitness goals on this day. If not, state what you will do tomorrow to meet them.

STANDARDIZED SERVING SIZES

One serving equals any of the following:

Fruit

- Any whole piece of fruit the size of a tennis ball
- 1 cup of cubed or balled fresh fruit, whole berries, or grapes
- $\frac{1}{2}$ cup diced fruit, canned fruit in its own juice, or full-strength fruit juice
- $\frac{1}{4}$ cup dried fruit bits

Vegetables

- 4 cups of raw salad greens
- 1 cup of raw, coarsely chopped or sliced vegetables
- $\frac{1}{2}$ cup cooked vegetables, all-vegetable soup, stewed tomatoes, or salsa
- 8 raw pieces the size of an index finger or chunks the size of cherry tomatoes

*G*rains

- 1 ounce slice of whole-grain bread, roll, tortilla, or muffin
- $^1/_2$ cup cooked whole grain or cereal or pasta
- $^3/_4$ cup ready-to-eat whole-grain cereal flakes, buds, or squares
- $^1/_4$ cup wheat germ or Grape Nuts
- $^1/_3$ cup granola or muesli
- 6 whole-grain crackers

*C*alcium-*R*ich *F*oods

- See the Calcium-to-Calories Connection on page 64 or use an amount that provides 200 to 300 mgs. of calcium.

R E L A T I V E F O O D P O R T I O N S

To help you out when you're eating away from home:

*M*easuring without a *R*uler

First joint of index finger . . . $^1/_2$ teaspoon or 1 inch

First joint (or tip) of thumb . . . 1 teaspoon

Tight fist . . . 1 cup

Palm of hand (diameter and thickness) . . . 3 ounces

Flat hand with closed fingers . . . 6 ounces

Spread fingers, from tip of thumb to tip of pinkie . . . 9 inches

Size and Dimension of Familiar Objects

Dollar bill . . . 6 $\frac{1}{4}$ inches long

Folded dollar bill . . . 3 $\frac{1}{8}$ inches long

American quarter . . . 1 inch diameter

Standard paper clip . . . 1 $\frac{1}{4}$ inches long

Big paper clip . . . 1 $\frac{7}{8}$ inches long

Tennis ball or baseball . . . 2 $\frac{1}{2}$ inches in diameter or 1 cup

Food and Object Comparisons

4 standard gaming dice . . . 1 ounce of cheese or meat cubes

3 $\frac{1}{2}$-inch computer disc . . . 1 ounce slice of cheese

Matchbook . . . 1 ounce of meat or cheese

Ping-Pong ball . . . 1 ounce meatball

Golf ball . . . 2 tablespoons peanut butter or cream cheese

3 ice cubes . . . $\frac{1}{2}$ cup rice or chopped vegetables

Deck of cards . . . 3 ounces meat, poultry, fish

Cassette tape case . . . 3 ounces meat, poultry, fish

Computer mouse . . . 4 ounces meat, poultry, fish

Bath bar of soap . . . 4 ounces meat, poultry, fish

300-page paperback book . . . 8 ounces meat, poultry, fish

Kitchen Science

1 cup = 8 fluid ounces or 16 tablespoons

1 pint = 2 cups

1 quart = 4 cups

THE WEDDING DRESS DIET

The Wedding Dress Diet Food and Fitness Log

Day __Saturday__   Date __July 17, 1999__

Time	Amount	Description of Food	Special Features	Calories	Fruit	Veg	Grain	Calcium
8³⁰ AM	1/2 c	cottage cheese	1% low fat	90				1
	1/2	cantaloupe		75	1			
	1/4 c	wheat germ		100			1	
	12 oz	coffee	brewed	0				
	2 tbsp	milk	1% low/fat	15				1/8
10 AM	6"	banana		100	1			
11 AM	12 oz	water		0				
12³⁰ pm	8"	tortilla	spinach				1 1/4	
	2 oz	turkey breast		80				
	1/2 c	sprouts		5		1/2		

TOTALS: _____

The Wedding Dress Diet Food and Fitness Log

Day _Saturday_ Date _July 17, 1999_

Time	Amount	Description of Food	Special Features	Calories	Fruit	Veg	Grain	Calcium
	½ C	Roasted Peppers		5		½		
	¼ C	Cheddar cheese	shredded	100				1
	12 oz	Lemonade	sugar free	0				
2:00 pm	6 oz	Hot cocoa	sugar free & fortified	50				1
	.75 oz	granola bar	low fat	110			1	
ETC.								
			TOTALS:					

Aerobic Activity _Cross Trainer_ Duration _45 min_ Exercise Heart Rate _140 bpm_

Resistance Exercises: Upper Body _yes_ Lower Body _yes_ Abs _yes_

Supplements taken? (Yes)/No Goals reached? Yes/(No)

If not, what will you do differently tomorrow? _drink more water with meals_

1 tablespoon = 3 teaspoons
2 tablespoons = 1 fluid ounce
6 teaspoons = 1 fluid ounce

1 stick butter/margarine = 4 ounces or $\frac{1}{2}$ cup or 8 tablespoons
1 cup shredded cheese = $\frac{1}{4}$ pound or 4 ounces
2 large raw eggs without shells = $\frac{1}{2}$ cup
1 cup ice cream = 5 ounces

2 ounces dry spaghetti = 1 cup cooked
2 ounces dry macaroni, penne, ziti = 1 $\frac{1}{4}$ cups cooked
1 cup dry long grain rice = 3 cups cooked
1 cup quick-cooking rice = 2 cups cooked
$\frac{1}{4}$ cup dry popcorn = 5 cups popped
1 pound nuts in shells = 1 $\frac{1}{2}$ to 2 cups shelled nuts
1 pound raw meat = 2 cups cooked, chopped meat

CHAPTER FIVE

EXERCISING FOR RESULTS

When most people talk about their "workout," they are referring to the gym they belong to, or the equipment they use, or the activity they prefer. You rarely hear them describe how much it's like a job, or "work," but that's exactly what exercise is.

If you think just showing up at a step class qualifies as a "workout," you're wrong. If you think donning your sneakers and taking a walk on your lunch hour is a "workout," you're wrong, too. And if you think you can miss a "workout" because you stayed out too late last night, you're wrong again.

To lose weight, your exercise regimen, or workout, must be

approached with the same seriousness you use to tackle any tough job. It doesn't matter whether you're having fun or feel like doing it. You've got to get results (read: lose weight and sculpt muscles), and that means making every session count.

If you were positioning yourself for a promotion at your job or a scholarship to graduate school, you wouldn't leave anything up to chance, right? One typo on your resumé can cancel out everything you've worked so hard to accomplish. When you want to be noticed and get ahead, you must always be on time and properly prepared. That applies to your workouts, too.

Have a plan of action and work your plan. Know where you started and where you want to end up. If you're doing a routine and don't see the desired loss of inches or pounds after a month, stop doing it and start something else that pays you for your effort.

Now for some startling statistics. You have around 600 muscles in your body, with about 400 of them affecting your physique. It is not possible to grow new muscles once you reach adulthood, any more than it is possible to grow taller. But you can tone, shape, and strengthen your muscles. The most fit and firm athlete must continually work her muscles or they will shrink and soften. There is no escaping the demands of a muscle. You must use it or lose it.

More frightening for most of us is the fact that there are anywhere between 25 to 75 *billion* fat cells in the body! Your genetic makeup determines where those fat cells are located, and nothing short of liposuction (which we don't recommend) can remove them. Fortunately, you can control how much fat you store in them. Eating an appropriate number of calories while doing regular, vigorous exercise will shrink those fat cells. But if and when you abandon that winning combination, your fat cells will engorge again.

PICK YOUR PASSION

In Chapter Four, you selected an activity factor to help you determine how many calories a day you can consume to reach your weight goal. Now you must choose the activity(ies) you will engage in every week to satisfy that time commitment. The activity(ies) will be the *aerobic*, or calorie-burning, part of your workout.

You must be able to perform each activity for at least thirty minutes and maintain your target heart rate while doing it. Be prepared to change the intensity of your workout if your heart rate is too fast or too slow. Whatever you do, don't become complacent. Anything that feels too easy or too comfortable might not be "work" anymore. Switch to something new to you or you're not so good at yet to be sure the time you put in produces the desired results.

There is no one value for energy expenditure that applies to everyone who does a particular exercise. The calories used when exercising are directly related to body weight. A heavier person will expend more energy than a lighter one if both are doing the same activity at the same intensity.

The list beginning on page 88 tells you the number of calories burned by women of different weights when performing each activity for one minute. You need to find the weight closest to yours, then look for the exercise you do, or plan to do. The number that intersects your weight and the exercise activity is the number of calories you use per minute while doing that activity. Multiply it by the number of minutes you do the exercise to see how many calories you used up. To lose weight, you should shoot for an aerobic exercise goal of burning the same number of calories in one week as you consume in one day. That means if you are eating 1,600 calories per day, you should select exercises, and enough exercise time, to expend 1,600 calories a week.

Another way you can maximize the amount of fat you burn during each workout is to exercise for as long as possible in each session. This allows your fat cells to release their stored deposits because your short-term body fuels, like glucose, cannot cover the longer work sessions. The longer you work out, the more conditioned your fat cells will become to dumping their stored fat into your bloodstream so it can be used as fuel.

To continue exercising for more than thirty minutes, you need to keep intensity at a moderate level. Again, use your heart rate as a guide to whether you are working too hard (more information about calculating your exercise heart rate can be found following the activity charts). It is also important to recognize that sweat is not a measure of how hard you're working. It simply means your body's internal temperature is heating up and you are cooling yourself off. Some people—such as most guys—just have an inordinate number of sweat glands, and they can soak a T-shirt without even trying. Use the clock and your heart rate to evaluate your performance.

If you haven't been exercising regularly and are over the age of thirty-five with more than thirty pounds to lose, consult your physician before beginning any exercise program.

CALORIES USED PER MINUTE FOR DIFFERENT ACTIVITIES

See the following charts.

CALORIC EXPENDITURES PER MINUTE BY ACTIVITY
Body Weights (in pounds)

ACTIVITY	110	123	139	150	163	176	190	203
AEROBIC DANCE								
Low intensity/impact	4.5	5.0	5.6	6.1	6.7	7.2	7.7	8.0
High intensity/impact	9.2	10.4	11.5	12.6	13.7	14.8	15.9	17.0
AQUA-RUNNING								
W/ floatation belt								
48/strides/minute	7.3	8.2	9.0	9.9	10.8	11.7	12.5	13.4
BENCH-STEPPING								
30 step cycle/minute								
6-in. bench	7.1	7.9	8.8	9.7	10.5	11.4	12.2	13.1
10-in. bench	8.5	9.5	10.5	11.5	12.5	13.5	14.5	15.6
BICYCLING—ROAD								
10–12 mph	5.3	5.9	6.5	7.1	7.8	8.4	9.0	9.7
14–16 mph	8.8	9.8	10.9	11.9	13.0	14.0	15.1	16.1

(Source: Calorie Expenditure Charts by Frank Katch, Victor Katch, and William McArdle; Fitness Technologies Press, 1996)

ACTIVITY	Body Weights (in pounds) (cont.)							
	110	123	139	150	163	176	190	203
STATIONARY BICYCLING								
60 rpm								
50 watts	3.4	3.8	4.2	4.6	5.0	5.4	5.9	6.3
100 watts	5.0	5.6	6.2	6.8	7.4	8.0	8.6	9.2
150 watts	6.6	7.4	8.2	8.9	9.7	10.5	11.3	12.1
CALISTHENICS								
Home, general, moderate	3.9	4.4	4.9	5.4	5.8	6.3	6.8	7.2
Vigorous	7.0	7.8	8.7	9.5	10.4	11.2	12.0	12.9
DANCE								
Ballroom—fast—and modern—swing, twist	5.3	5.9	6.5	7.1	7.8	8.4	9.0	9.7
Big Band, rock 'n' roll	4.2	4.7	5.2	5.7	6.2	6.7	7.2	7.7

Body Weights (in pounds) (cont.)

ACTIVITY	110	123	139	150	163	176	190	203
EQUESTRIAN								
Trotting horseback	5.7	6.4	7.1	7.7	8.4	9.1	9.8	10.5
Galloping	7.0	7.8	8.7	9.5	10.4	11.2	12.0	12.9
GYMNASTICS								
General	3.5	3.9	4.3	4.8	5.2	5.6	6.0	6.4
ICE-SKATING								
Less than 9 mph	4.8	5.4	6.0	6.5	7.1	7.7	8.3	8.9
More than 9 mph	7.9	8.8	9.8	10.7	11.7	12.6	13.5	14.5
JAZZERCISE								
Moderate	5.8	6.5	7.2	7.9	8.5	9.2	9.9	10.6
W/6x8-in. bench, music 120 beats/min.	7.7	8.6	9.5	10.4	11.3	12.3	13.2	14.1

	Body Weights (in pounds) (cont.)									
ACTIVITY	**110**	**123**	**139**	**150**	**163**	**176**	**190**	**203**		
KICKBOXING	8.8	9.9	11.0	12.0	13.1	14.1	15.2	16.3		
MINI TRAMPOLINE										
120 foot strikes/min.										
No arm pumping, weights, or jumping	6.9	7.7	8.5	9.4	10.2	11.0	11.8	12.7		
Arms pumping, holding 1-lb. hand weights, 2-ft. jumping	8.7	9.7	10.8	11.8	12.9	13.9	15.0	16.0		
ROLLER-SKATING										
Inside, rink	5.7	6.4	7.1	7.7	8.4	9.1	10.1	10.8		
Outside, pavement	6.2	7.0	7.7	8.4	9.2	9.9	10.7	11.4		
ROLLERBLADING										
Casual	6.7	7.4	8.2	9.0	9.8	10.6	11.4	12.2		
Vigorous—12.4 mph on asphalt	10.6	11.9	13.1	14.4	15.7	16.9	18.2	19.5		

Body Weights (in pounds) (cont.)

ACTIVITY	110	123	139	150	163	176	190	203
ROWING (On Concept II Ergometer)								
50 watts, 16/mph								
age 20–29	4.0	4.4	4.9	5.4	5.9	6.4	6.8	7.3
age 30–39	3.6	4.0	4.4	4.8	5.3	5.7	6.1	6.5
age 40–49	3.4	3.8	4.2	4.6	5.0	5.4	5.8	6.2
110 watts, 16/mph								
age 20–29	7.3	8.2	9.0	9.4	9.9	10.2	10.9	11.7
age 30–39	7.3	8.2	9.0	9.9	10.8	11.6	12.5	13.4
age 40–49	6.8	7.7	8.5	9.3	10.8	11.6	12.5	13.4
STATIONARY ERGOMETER								
General	8.3	9.3	10.3	11.3	12.3	13.3	14.3	15.3

	Body Weights (in pounds) (cont.)							
ACTIVITY	110	123	139	150	163	176	190	203
RUNNING								
6 mph, 10 min./hr. pace	8.8	9.8	10.9	11.9	13.0	14.0	15.1	16.1
8.6 mph, 7 min./hr. pace	12.3	13.7	15.2	16.7	18.1	19.6	21.1	22.5
In water, 1.3 m. deep, no vest, maximum effort	15.0	16.8	18.6	20.4	22.2	24.0	25.8	27.5
Jog-walk combo (jog portion less than 10 mins.)	5.3	5.9	6.5	7.1	7.8	8.4	9.0	9.7
SKIING MACHINES								
NordicTrack (general)	8.3	9.3	10.3	11.3	12.3	13.3	14.3	15.3
SLIDE BOARD								
66-in.-wide board done to 40 slides/min.	7.7	8.7	9.6	10.5	11.4	12.4	13.3	14.2

Body Weights (in pounds) (cont.)

ACTIVITY	110	123	139	150	163	176	190	203
STAIR-CLIMBING								
LifeStep 78% max. heart rate	6.3	7.0	7.8	8.5	9.3	10.0	10.8	11.5
StairMaster 4000								
30 steps/min.	6.1	6.9	7.6	8.3	9.1	9.8	10.5	11.3
46–48 steps/min.	8.8	9.8	10.9	11.9	13.0	14.0	15.1	16.1
SWIMMING								
Slow crawl, 50 yds./min.	7.0	7.8	8.7	9.5	10.4	11.2	12.0	12.9
Freestyle laps, vigorous effort	8.8	9.8	10.9	11.9	13.0	14.0	15.1	16.1
TAI CHI								
Skilled performers	3.6	4.0	4.4	4.9	5.3	5.7	6.2	6.6
TAE KWAN DO	8.2	9.2	10.2	11.2	12.2	13.2	14.1	15.1

	Body Weights (in pounds) (cont.)							
ACTIVITY	**110**	**123**	**139**	**150**	**163**	**176**	**190**	**203**
TENNIS—RECREATIONAL								
Doubles	6.1	6.9	7.6	8.3	9.1	9.8	10.5	11.3
Singles	7.0	7.8	8.7	9.5	10.4	11.2	12.0	12.9
TRAMPOLINE—RECREATIONAL	3.1	3.4	3.8	4.2	4.5	4.9	5.3	5.6
WALKING—GENERAL								
3.0 mph, level, firm surface	3.1	3.4	3.8	4.2	4.5	4.9	5.3	5.6
4.0 mph, level, firm surface	3.5	3.9	4.3	4.8	5.2	5.6	6.0	6.4
Wearing 1-lb. hand weight at 70% max. heart rate	7.8	8.7	9.6	10.6	11.5	12.4	13.4	14.3
RACE-WALKING								
6 mph	9.6	10.8	11.9	13.1	14.2	15.4	16.6	17.7
8 mph	14.0	15.7	17.4	19.0	20.7	22.4	24.1	25.8

Body Weights (in pounds) (cont.)									
ACTIVITY	110	123	139	150	163	176	190	203	
TREADMILL									
3 mph, no incline	4.0	4.5	4.9	5.4	5.9	6.4	6.9	7.3	
4 mph, no incline	5.1	5.8	6.4	7.0	7.6	8.2	8.8	9.5	
YOGA	3.0	3.3	3.7	4.0	4.4	4.8	5.1	5.5	
RESISTANCE TRAINING									
General circuit w/ machines	7.0	7.8	8.7	9.5	10.4	11.2	12.0	12.9	
Universal Gym	6.1	6.9	7.6	8.3	9.0	9.7	10.5	11.2	
Nautilus—12 exercises, 8.12 reps @ 14–19 min. duration	4.1	4.6	5.1	5.6	6.1	6.6	7.1	7.6	

Body Weights (in pounds) (cont.)

ACTIVITY	110	123	139	150	163	176	190	203
SPORTS AND FUN								
Badminton	3.9	4.4	4.9	5.4	5.8	6.3	6.8	7.2
Basketball—nongame, shooting around	5.3	5.9	6.5	7.1	7.8	8.4	9.0	9.7
Bowling	2.6	2.9	3.3	3.6	3.9	4.2	4.5	4.8
Darts—wall or lawn	2.2	2.5	2.7	3.0	3.2	3.5	3.8	4.0
Frisbee	2.6	2.9	3.3	3.6	3.9	4.2	4.5	4.8
Golf								
General	3.9	4.4	4.9	5.4	5.8	6.3	6.8	7.2
Miniature	2.6	2.9	3.3	3.6	3.9	4.2	4.5	4.8
Juggling	3.5	3.9	4.3	4.8	5.2	5.6	6.0	6.4
Racquetball—casual	6.1	6.9	7.6	8.3	9.1	9.8	10.5	11.3
Soccer—casual	6.1	6.9	7.6	8.3	9.1	9.8	10.5	11.3
Softball—fast or slow pitch	4.4	4.9	5.4	6.0	6.5	7.0	7.5	8.1
Table tennis/Ping-Pong	3.5	3.9	4.3	4.8	5.2	5.6	6.0	6.4
Volleyball								
Beach	6.1	6.9	7.6	8.3	9.1	9.8	10.5	11.3
Indoors	2.6	2.9	3.3	3.6	3.9	4.4	4.7	5.0

CALCULATING YOUR EXERCISE
HEART RATE

If your age and corresponding exercise heart rate are not included in the chart on page 65 in Chapter Four, you can calculate the value yourself. Here's how:

---

1. Determine your maximum heart rate by subtracting your age from 220:

$$220 - \underline{\hspace{2cm}} = \underline{\hspace{3cm}}$$
     your age   **max heart rate**

2. Multiply the number you get by the percentages below for heart rate zones:

Start-up rate = _____ × **.55 =** _____ **beats per minute**
         max heart rate

Intermediate = _____ × **.65 =** _____ **beats per minute**
         max heart rate

Experienced = _____ × **.75 =** _____ **beats per minute**
         max heart rate

SHAPE, TONE, AND DEFINE
THOSE MUSCLES

You took all those measurements of yourself back in Chapter One, remember? Now it's time to adjust the numbers a bit.

Exercising for Results

Losing pounds is only part of the solution to your figure flaws. Adding and subtracting inches are equally important.

Instead of aiming for the smallest waist possible or the tightest butt in the gym, you should instead focus on balancing your body proportions. Big hips don't look nearly as wide when matched by broad shoulders. That's why fashion designers put shoulder pads in jackets and dresses. Shapely, muscular calves draw the eye away from thick thighs. That's what high-heeled shoes have always done for women, in addition to killing our feet!

As discussed in Chapter Three, the "X" in the H-O-A-X figure categories is based on the notion that to achieve the "classic" hourglass figure, a woman's bust and hip measurement should be about the same, with a waistline ten inches smaller. Take a look at your measurements and decide which have to be built up or scaled down to achieve these proportions. Then select some shaping, toning, and defining exercises from the chart on page 104 to achieve those results.

Even if you're well proportioned or at your healthy body weight, flabby arms, jiggly thighs, or a pot belly may still be a problem. You, too, must do some shaping, toning, and defining exercises to control the loose flesh that will be revealed in an off-the-shoulder bridal gown or honeymoon bikini.

Then there are women who aren't really flabby—they just lack definition. You know who you are. Maybe your arms are tubular, your back is square, and/or your calves straight. Well, that's all right if you're Mrs. Potato Head, but ideally, real bodies have muscles with shapes and curves. You can use the shaping, toning, and defining exercises to chisel out some curves in your muscles just like a sculptor does in marble.

With the recommended exercises, you have the option of doing them at home with no special equipment, using inexpensive dumbbells and barbells, or working out with freestanding resistance equipment. You can also take advantage of some common household items to help you with your workouts. One-pound soup cans (with the soup still inside, of course) can fill in for one-pound hand weights or dumbbells. A sturdy wooden box or the lower step in a staircase can serve as a bench. A chair back can replace the ballet barre, and a ten-inch rubber ball can be used as a squeeze ball.

THE TRUTH ABOUT CELLULITE

Some thin people have cellulite and some fat people don't— sort of like freckles. And as much as the cosmetics industry would like you to believe you can rub a cream onto your thighs and make cellulite disappear, it's never going to happen, any more than you can wash away your freckles.

Cellulite is a dimpling of the skin caused by connective tissue stretching over fat cells. One of the ways to minimize the dimpling is to shrink the size of those fat cells so the connective tissue doesn't have to stretch so far. And isn't that just what you're trying to do anyway?

In addition to shrinking the fat cells, you also need to strengthen the muscles in the area of the dimpling, typically the hips, thighs, and butt. Strong muscles are more rigid, which allows them to pull and smooth out the layer of fat, connective tissue, and skin that lies on top of them.

EXERCISES TO SHAPE, TONE, AND DEFINE

The floor work exercises we refer to in the chart on page 104 are the ones you can do using your own body weight for resistance. For example, when you do a push-up, it's just you and your muscles down there on the floor. By using proper form and the right number of sets and repetitions, you can get results that are as good as when exercise equipment is used.

Most of these exercises can also be done using free weights, like dumbbells and barbells or ankle and wrist weights. The common household items mentioned earlier can also be used as substitutes. By adding weights to your workout, you can control the amount of resistance applied to a particular muscle and get better shaping and definition.

Resistance equipment is the stuff that you may find in your kid brother's bedroom or your fiancé's basement. A multipurpose bench, universal gym, fixed weight machines, or Nautilus and Cybex equipment fall into this category. Any gym or fitness center you go to will be filled with the stuff.

Descriptions of the most basic exercises you can do without free weights or resistance equipment to shape, tone, and define your muscles are provided in the section How to Do It beginning on page 103. If you have your own "heavy metal" or a gym membership, follow the instructions for form and technique provided with each piece you work out with.

DO IT RIGHT OR DON'T DO IT AT ALL

One of the most common mistakes made when doing toning and resistance exercises is going too fast. The action, or *work*, should be very slow and deliberate so you can isolate the involved muscle and contract it through the entire motion, then slowly release it. There should be no bounce and swing in the movement, just a slow, concentrated contraction. If done properly, you won't be able to do as many repetitions, but you'll see results a lot sooner.

And remember, *exhale* on the exertion. Breathing during the exertion ensures that blood flow will not be blocked when you are working the muscle, which can lead to cramping. The abdominal muscles also contract when exhaling, which helps strengthen the abs in their flattened position.

As important as your speed is your form. Just because you're working on your biceps doesn't mean the rest of your muscles get to take a siesta. Before each exercise you must get into proper position. If standing, are your feet and legs shoulder-width apart with weight equally distributed? Are your shoulders squarely over your hips? Is your stomach pulled in? If you remember to check your alignment before each repetition, you'll get the benefit of toning all those other muscle groups while specifically working the one.

The American College of Sports Medicine recommends that weight training be done at least three days a week and that you let muscles rest a day between training sessions. Four to five exercises should be done for both the upper and lower body muscles. Each set should include ten to fifteen repetitions, with one to two sets per workout.

HOW TO DO IT

Many an injury has occurred in otherwise fit people who ignore the fundamental rules of exercise. Do not take short cuts. Use all exercise equipment properly or you risk being side-lined in these crucial weeks before the ceremony when you can least afford to be wrapped in Ace bandages or hobbling on crutches.

Abdominal crunch: Lie on back with knees bent, feet flat on floor and hip-width apart, stomach muscles tight. Place hands

Muscle	Free Style*	Resistance Equipment
SHOULDERS	Shrugs	Lateral raises
UPPER BACK	Deltoid push-up	Back extension
CHEST	Push-up	Butterfly machine
TRICEPS in the back of the upper arm	Bench dip	Bench press
BICEPS in the front of the upper arm	Bicep curl	Lateral pulldown
UPPER ABS	Trunk curl	Ab press
LOWER ABS	Crunch	Ab press
BUTTOCKS	Donkey kicks	Kneeling leg curl
HIPS	Side squats	Hip machine
THIGHS	Wall squat	Adduction/abduction machines
QUADRICEPS large muscle in front of thigh	Lunges	Leg extension
HAMSTRING	Arabesque	Seated leg curl
CALVES	Heel raises and toe-ups	Leg presses
WAIST	Side bends	Rotary torso

*These exercises are described on the following pages. They can be done with or without hand weights.

behind your head, fingertips touching, but not linked. Keep elbows straight out to the sides of your head the entire time. Tuck chin slightly. Now slowly pull up your head, neck, shoulders, and chest in one movement, pausing once your upper back is raised off the floor, then slowly lower yourself to the starting position. Repeat 8 to 12 times.

Arabesque: Use a high-back chair for this exercise. Stand with feet hip-width apart and chair back in front of you an arm's length away. Slowly extend your left leg straight back, tightening the glutteal (rump or buttocks) muscles as you raise your leg until it is 8 to 12 inches off the floor. Now slightly bend the knee to lift the heel toward your butt, while maintaining the contraction in the upper leg. Hold for 10 seconds, then extend the leg and slowly bring it back to the starting position. Repeat 8 to 12 times, then do the other leg. *Tips:* Do a posture check—head up, shoulders and hips aligned, tummy pulled in.

Bench dips: Find a bench or sturdy chair to use with this exercise. Sit on the edge of the bench with your legs together straight in front of you, toes pointing up. Grip the bench behind you with the heels of your hands. Keep your elbows relaxed, then slide your behind off the seat and support your weight with your arms. Slowly bend your elbows to lower your body until your upper arms are parallel to the floor behind you. Now slowly raise yourself back up again without settling back onto the seat. Repeat 8 to 12 times. *Tips:* Keep your shoulders down and your back straight. Do not let your shoulders rise toward your ears. For greater resistance, put your feet on a box in front of you.

Bicep curls: Use two one-pound cans or dumbbells for this exercise. Stand with feet shoulder-width apart, holding one weight in each hand with palms facing up. Pull the upper arms close to the body and pinch the elbows into your waist. Slowly raise your hands up to your shoulders, hold that position, then slowly lower your arms to your sides. Repeat 8 to 12 times. *Tips:* Do not jerk the weights up, then let them flop down. Isolate the bicep muscles in your upper arms and pull the weights up using them.

Deltoid push-up: Make your body into a bridge, bending at the waist, with your butt in the air, hands flat on the floor shoulder-width apart and legs together with your toes down and heels raised. Slowly lower your head to the floor by bending your elbows, hold the position, then slowly raise yourself back to the starting position. Repeat 8-12 times. *Tips:* Keep your elbows slightly bent, even when your head is fully raised. Keep your body bent at the same angle while lowering and raising your weight.

Donkey kick: Get down on all fours on a padded carpet or exercise mat. Rest your weight on your forearms, with your palms down. Slowly pull your left knee into your chest, keeping your back straight—do not arch or cave your back. Now slowly extend that leg out and above your buttocks pushing your heel toward the ceiling. Hold the position, then slowly bring the leg back under your body without putting your weight on it. Repeat 10 to 20 times, then do the other leg. *Tips:* Pull in your stomach to keep your back from sagging. Keep your head up and your neck aligned with your spine.

Forward lunges: Stand with feet together, hands on hips. Extend left foot about two feet in front of you, planting your foot firmly on the floor, toes forward. Slowly lower your body to bring the right knee toward the floor. Keep your head up and your back straight. Stop when the knee of the front leg is at a right angle. Hold that position, then slowly raise your body up and bring in the front leg to the starting position. Repeat 8 to 12 times, then do the other leg. *Tips:* Squeeze your buttocks together and pull in your stomach with each lunge. Keep your head up and look straight in front of you, not at the floor.

Heel raises and toe-ups: Stand with feet together, hips and shoulders aligned. Hold onto a wall or chair back for balance. Raise your heels and curl onto your toes while tightening the buttocks and abdominal muscles. Hold for 3 to 5 seconds. Then lower to starting position. Repeat 10 to 20 times. Now flex your feet, raising your toes while you rock back onto your heels. Hold for 3 to 5 seconds. Return to start position. Repeat 10 to 20 times. *Tips:* Tighten your buttocks and abdominal muscles as you raise and lower yourself. Don't look down. Keep your chest and head up.

Push-ups (beginners): Lie on your stomach on a padded carpet or exercise mat. Place your hands underneath each shoulder, palms down. Bend your knees, about 8 to 10 inches apart, and cross your ankles in the air. Now slowly straighten your arms to lift your torso off the floor, keeping your weight balanced on your hands and knees. Pause once your body is raised, then slowly lower yourself until your upper arms are parallel to the floor—do not go all the way back to the starting position. Repeat 8 to 12 times. *Tips:* Keep back straight throughout the exercise. Tighten abs to support back and keep chin tucked.

Shoulder shrugs: Use two one-pound cans or dumbbells. Stand with feet hip-width apart, shoulders relaxed, arms down at your sides, holding one weight in each hand. Slowly raise your shoulders straight up toward your ears, hold the position, then slowly lower them again. Repeat 10 to 20 times. *Tips:* Tuck buttocks beneath you and slightly tilt hips back. Exhale as you raise your shoulders, inhale when you lower them.

Side bends: Use a one-pound can or dumbbell. Stand with feet shoulder-width apart, left arm at your side holding the weight. Put your right hand behind your head with your elbow sticking straight out from your ear. Bending at the waist, slowly slide your left hand toward the floor without tipping forward or shifting your pelvis. Your right elbow should point toward the ceiling as you dip to the left. Bend to the lowest point you can reach, hold, then slowly come up to the starting position. Repeat 10 to 20 times, then do the other side. *Tips:* Keep shoulders square and stomach pulled in. Proper form is more important than how far you can dip.

Side squats: Stand with legs hip-width apart, feet facing forward, not turned out. Extend arms straight in front of you for balance, or rest them on your hips. Squat down about 8 to 12 inches by slowly bending the knees without tipping forward. Now step out to the left as far as you can, still holding the squat position. Pull the right leg over next to the left while in the squat, then slowly return to a standing position. Now repeat the movement, stepping out to the right first and bringing in your left leg. Repeat 10 to 12 times. *Tips:* Keep toes facing front at all times. Do not bounce down and up; control the movement from start to finish.

Trunk curl: Lie on your back on a carpet or padded mat. Bend your knees and pull your feet in toward your butt. Now drop your knees out to the sides and put the soles of your feet together. Position your arms over the front of your body with your hands crossed over your waist. Slowly curl your shoulders and back off the floor without jerking your neck, and reach toward your ankles with your hands. Only your upper back should rise off the floor. Hold the position 10 seconds, then slowly lower your shoulders until your head is just above the floor. Repeat 8 to 12 times. *Tips:* Keep your head aligned with your spine and your chin up. Do not use your head and neck to pull yourself up.

Wall squats: Stand about one foot away from the wall with hands on hips. Lean back against the wall making sure head, shoulders, and lower back are touching it. Slowly lower backside down the wall until you are in a sitting position with your knees at right angles. Hold the position, then slowly raise yourself up again without moving your feet or pulling away from the wall. Repeat 8 to 12 times. *Tips:* Keep weight evenly distributed on both legs to maintain balance. Don't lurch forward or remove head from contact with wall.

WORKING OUT WITH OTHERS

There is no one perfect time or place to work out. Different people have different tastes in this, just as they do with diamond settings. But if you are thinking about joining a gym, there are some things you should consider before signing on.

First, how convenient is the gym to your home or job? You're going to have to get there three or four times a week. It better be on the way to or from the place you travel to each day or you may never make it. Next, what are the hours of operation? If you're an early riser, be sure they open early.

Beware of being oversold on the juice bar, tanning salon, child care services, and herbal shampoos if you have no intention of using them. If you're into classes like spinning or kickboxing, check out when they are scheduled, then visit when you're most likely to attend to see how crowded they are. If you're mainly interested in using the aerobic and resistance equipment, visit when you're likely to be using the gym and note how long the wait is to get on the pieces you want.

If you're thinking of hiring a personal trainer, the best way to find a good one is through direct referral from someone who has used a trainer and been satisfied with the results. Once you have a name or two, be sure to verify that the person is certified through the American College of Sports Medicine (ACSM) or the American Council on Exercise (ACE) or the National Strength and Conditioning Association (NCSA). The phone numbers for these three organizations are listed in the next section.

One of the best ways to stick to a workout program is to do it with an exercise buddy. Look at your Wedding Dress Diet Contract to see if one of your "supporters" is also someone who can work out with you. Once you've made a commitment to someone else to show up on the corner for that early-morning bike ride, or for regular Saturday-afternoon Rollerblading in the park, or for a lunchtime visit to the fitness center in your office building, you'll be less likely to procrastinate about exercising. You have a date with someone and that's the commitment you keep, even if it's to go exercise.

RESOURCES AND PRODUCTS
WE LIKE

Organizations
- American College of Sports Medicine, (317) 637-9200 or http://www.ASCM.org
- American Council on Exercise, (800) 825-3636 or http://acefitness.org
- National Strength and Conditioning Association, (719) 632-6722 or http://www.ncsa-lift.org

Music and videos:
- Collage Video—home exercise videos featuring aerobics, step, toning, yoga, and much more, (800) 433-6769 or http://www.collagevideo.com
- Sports Music, Inc.—exercise tapes for all styles of music and every fitness level, (800) 878-4764 or http://www.sportsmusic.com

Fitness equipment:
- Aquajogger Aquafit Barbells, Webbed Pro Gloves, and Fit Buoyance Belt, (800) 922-9544 or http://www.aqua jogger.com
- Eastbay—sports apparel and footwear, (800) 826-2205 or http://www.eastbay.com
- Exercise at about.com—links to many equipment retailers plus lots of information about fitness and training, http://exercise.about.com

- Fitness Link—product reviews, suggestions on what to look for when selecting equipment, plus links to dealers, http://www.fitnesslink.com
- Freestyle Sports Watches and Accessories—high-performance, all-sport watches, heart rate monitors, and accessories "that look as great as they perform," (877) 789-5325 or http://freestyleusa.com
- IDEA, an organization of fitness professionals; see "Fitness Links" for fitness equipment and heart rate monitors, http://www.ideafit.com
- Polar Heart Rate Monitor—several models and price ranges available, (800) 227-1314 or http://www.polarusa.com
- Road Runner Sports—bills itself as the world's largest running shoe site with more than 130,000 shoes available, (800) 551-5558 or http://www.roadrunnersports.com
- Speedo Surf Runner Radio, Swimfoil Paddles, (888) 477-3336 or http://www.speedo.com
- Title 9 Sports—sports bras and women's athletic apparel, (800) 609-0092 or http://www.title9sports.com
- Yamax Digi-Walker—excellent pedometer/step counter; one retail source is at http://www.pedometers.com

POINTERS ON POSTURE

Without counting a single calorie or lifting a single dumbbell, you can lose five pounds. That is, the *illusion* of five lost pounds, but who's to know? The secret is good posture.

Ever catch your reflection in a store window or department store mirror and suddenly adjust yourself? If you answered "yes," it's because you've seen how horrible the slumped shoulders and protruding belly look when you're slouching.

You can do something about that slouch, and get rid of it forever. And there will never be a better time in your life than right now as you get ready to take center stage on your wedding day. We're going to show you how.

Stand up with this book open in front of you and follow these simple instructions as you read them, then practice these steps every time you get up out of a chair or are standing for any length of time. You can condition your "posture muscles" to remember what to do, just like all those soldiers have done before you. Don't think for a minute they all showed up at boot camp with straight spines and tight buns. If you follow this advice, you'll never have to make an adjustment in front of the mirror again!

Starting at the top, imagine yourself balancing a book on your head. If you do, you will straighten your back, raise your chest, and ever so slightly lift the breasts.

Next, think about a swan or a graceful actress like Gwyneth

Paltrow as you elongate your neck. This keeps your chin up and prevents those dreadful doubles.

Now gently press your shoulders down and back to center them over your hips. Be sure your weight is evenly distributed over each foot.

Finally, gently tighten the buttocks, which will also cause you to pull in those abdominal muscles. Don't you feel lighter already?

EXERCISE MYTHS AND REALITIES

. . . *About atrophy*: This is the shrinking of a muscle due to lack of use. The point is, muscle cannot turn into fat. Lack of exercise reduces the size of your muscles while increasing the opportunity for fat storage.

. . . *About breathing*: Pay attention to your breathing when doing resistance exercises. Holding your breath when contracting a muscle causes you to push out the stomach muscles, which is where they're going to stay if you do it over and over. *Exhale* on the exertion and your stomach will compress.

. . . *About cooling down*: This is what you do at the end of an aerobic or a fast-paced resistance workout that raises heart rate. You're going to need that heart for the rest of your life. Give it a chance to return to a normal rhythm.

. . . *About dancing:* Ballroom, jitterbug, salsa—it's all aerobic and a fun way to work out with your future husband. Sign up for some dance lessons so you can strut your stuff at the wedding. And don't forget to do some discreet stretches before you get on that dance floor at the wedding or you'll be hobbling on your honeymoon!

. . . *About fingers:* They can get smaller when you lose weight, which will affect your ring size. Don't take a chance on losing your wedding band while waving good-bye to your family at the airport. Have your rings refitted and, if necessary, resized a few weeks before the big day.

. . . *About gear:* We're not talking fashion here, but practical, comfortable clothing and sneakers. Don't forget your wristwatch with a second-hand sweep, heart monitor, hair clips, weight gloves, and headset or portable music system.

. . . *About plateaus:* They happen, and they can be frustrating. The key to preventing them and breaking them is change. Vary your workouts by cross-training or doing circuit training. Break up long workouts by doing three different aerobic exercises for fifteen minutes each instead of just one for forty-five minutes. If you normally work out indoors, go outside and do something, or vice versa.

. . . *About reps:* As in repetitions, or how many times you repeat a particular exercise. Depending on your goal, you may increase your reps using a lighter resistance to tone a muscle, or limit the reps while using more resistance to increase the size of a muscle. The ideal number is one more than you can comfortably do with the given resistance. For example, when using a three-pound dumbbell to do bicep curls, if you can complete nine in proper form, and the tenth one takes maximum effort, stop at ten. Do more sets of these to tone, or increase the resistance and do fewer reps and sets to build muscles.

. . . *About sets:* How many times you repeat a series of exercises. For example, if you are working your upper body and doing six different exercises for eight to twelve reps each, doing two or three more sets will provide better definition of the targeted muscles.

. . . *About stretching:* Watch a cat sometime and you'll understand what this is all about: slow, easy movements that give the muscles a chance to elongate and arch and relax.

. . . *About warming up:* Do this before you start any type of workout. It's a necessary part of the exercise routine. Start moving all the large muscle groups in a rhythmic pattern, slowly at first, then gradually progressing in speed. Marching in place while pumping the arms or side steps while swinging the arms out to each side will get the heart pumping and the blood flowing to those muscles you're about to work.

... *About water:* Drink before you work out, while you work out, and after you're finished working out. Aim for one quart of water per hour of exercise.

EXERCISING WHILE DOING OTHER THINGS

If you want to lose pounds and inches as quickly as possible, the exercising you need to do is what we've prescribed so far. However, we realize that not *all* brides-to-be can fit in the time for serious exercise—if they have, say, a couple of kids to care for, or they're forced to work twelve-hour days at the office. If you're in a similar situation, you should incorporate what researchers call "lifestyle" exercise into your daily routine. Lifestyle exercise includes activities such as walking around the house during commercials, or parking farther out at the mall. Researchers at the Cooper Institute of Aerobics Research in Dallas recently concluded a study in which half of the participants spent twenty to sixty minutes per day up to five days a week vigorously exercising—swimming or bicycling, for example. The other half incorporated thirty minutes a day of lifestyle exercising. At the end of six months, researchers found that both groups had similar and significant improvements in cholesterol readings, blood pressure, and body fat percentages. But—and this is key—*the lifestyle exercisers had to exercise three times longer than those who vigorously exercised in order to burn the same number of calories.* But we're talking about the wimpy lifestyle stuff here, like walking around during commercials. The more vigorous tasks you perform regularly really can add points in your weekly calorie-burning goal. For example:

Housework burns. If you perform household tasks vigorously, you are getting beneficial exercise. Window washing, food shopping, or mopping burn 3.7 calories per minute. Sweeping or dusting uses 3.8 calories per minute. Waxing or scrubbing floors is good for 6.8 calories a minute. Vacuuming is a real workout: 7 calories per minute. Outside: Rake leaves—you'll burn 5 calories a minute. Remember, the key word here is *vigorously.*

TONERS

And here are some toners you can do while doing something else, as well:

For tightening the abdominal muscles to flatten your stomach. Jacqueline got this tip from fitness expert Sheila Cluff while visiting her fitness spa in Ojai, California: Just "hold it in." "Make it a habit of contracting your abdominal muscles whenever you think about it," Cluff said. "You can do this exercise any place and at any time—while cooking dinner, for example." Contract your stomach muscles for a slow count of ten, relax, and repeat, remembering to check and correct your posture at the same time and to breathe deeply.

To tone up the butt. Another tip from Sheila Cluff: Whenever you climb the stairs, pretend you're holding a gold coin between your cheeks and don't "drop" it till you reach the top. A woman we know does a variation of this: Whenever she's doing "hold it in" for her stomach, she also clenches her buttocks. She says she does this constantly when she's waiting in line. "As long as you're wearing a fairly full dress or a long loose-fitting skirt no one's the wiser!"

To trim the thighs. Do wall squats—described earlier in this chapter—while you're on the phone. And here's another one of Sheila Cluff's funny but effective ideas, as long as you have stairs: Waddle up the stairs with a wiggle like Charlie Chaplin, feet turned outward, your knees flexed, your pelvis tucked. This is excellent for the inner thighs.

And don't forget the most fun exercise-while-doing-something-else activity of all: **sex!** See Chapter Ten for the calorie-burning potential!

CHAPTER SIX

EATING BETWEEN FITTINGS

By this time, you're probably feeling overwhelmed by all that you still have to do, and underappreciated for all you have done so far. Eating right and exercising regularly may feel like more hassles in your already harried life. But you cannot give up!

Look at it this way: You *have* to eat, right? If you give in to temptation at every turn, you will have to deal with all the guilt and pounds that follow. If you keep your wits about you, you can go to bed at night knowing you are a few ounces closer to your wedding-day weight. That's sure to lead to pleasant dreams!

MEALS VERSUS SNACKS

The worst mistake you can make is to skip a meal to make time for one more errand. No one ever lost weight by skipping meals. In fact, most people gain weight from all the meals they don't eat. Why? Because something will eventually cross your lips in lieu of the missed bowl of cereal or cup of soup or plate of salad. And that something will more likely than not be something with more calories, fat, and sodium than the meal you passed up.

The problem stems from the arbitrary way people categorize food. We think that if it's "mealtime," we eat "meal food." And if it's "snack time" we eat "snack food."

Robyn has counseled many people who say they never have time for breakfast, yet they eat a stack of cookies around three in the afternoon "for a snack." It never occurs to them to have a frozen waffle with light syrup at three o'clock, or a dish of oatmeal with raisins—both of which are lower in fat and calories than the cookies. People are amazed to learn that the "meal" they missed first thing in the morning can still be eaten in the middle of the afternoon. It's not as if your stomach can tell what time it is, or that the Food Police will arrest you for eating "breakfast food" in the afternoon!

Another danger in skipping meals is that it is harder to keep track of all the "little" things you eat as snacks. Meals are eaten at a table or another traditional "eating place." You set out dishes and flatware in a ceremonial fashion, then place all the food in front of you. If you are eating with others, you're probably not doing anything else except talking while you eat. When you're finished, you have a pretty good idea of what you ate because you were paying attention to the food.

On the other hand, when you don't eat meals and instead snack your way through the day, you lose sight of what you have eaten within seconds after swallowing. That candy jar on the receptionist's desk empties out every couple of days, but no one wants to chip in to refill it, claiming "I never eat the stuff." Oh? Try going through your waste basket at the end of a day in which you skipped lunch. Count the food wrappers you find in there. Or look around your car after spending the day running to every shoe store and lingerie shop in town. There's bound to be evidence of food eaten that you have long since forgotten.

The bottom line is that foods gobbled up while talking on the phone, driving the car, and dashing through the mall are lethal. Because of convenience, such food is typically high in calories, fat, and sodium, and it's too easy to forget to add it to your food log. Trust us, you're better off eating meals.

Okay, so you're going to eat a meal away from home. Not

to put a bloody-bones-and-butcher-knives scare into you, but you have to be careful here, as well. In a recent study, researchers at the University of Memphis and Vanderbilt University found that women who eat more than five meals a week outside the home consume more calories, sodium, and fat than those who eat out less often. The researchers found that women who ate out more often consumed an average of 2,056 calories a day, 3,299 milligrams of sodium a day, and obtained nearly 35 percent of their daily calories from fat. The comparable data for the women who ate out less often: 1,768 calories, 2,902 milligrams of sodium, and 31 percent of calories from fat. When asked about the implications of this data, the researchers rather wimpily replied that "further research is needed to enhance healthful eating in restaurants." Well, you don't have time to wait for that.

KEEPING SCORE

If your schedule looks crazy and you fear you might end up eating meals on the fly, here's what to do:

1. Consider what your dining options are wherever you're going to be at a mealtime. Will you be in the mall, downtown, on the freeway, or dropping something off at a friend's house?

What kind of food services are available to you that might meet your needs?

2. Subtotal your food log for the day so far *before* you leave home, work, or wherever you've spent the first part of your day. How many calories do you have left to work with? How many servings of fruits and vegetables, whole grains, and calcium-rich dairy foods have you eaten so far?

3. Decide ahead of time where you will eat your next meal. Change your route or the order in which you do your errands to make it possible to be near an eatery that has suitable choices.

4. Plan your menu so you know exactly what you will order when you get there. Use the guidelines below to help make your decision.

5. Record the meal on your food log as soon as you finish eating, then go about your business.

When eating commercially prepared food, you not only have to watch out for jumbo portions that will push up your calorie count, but also many hidden sources of fat and way too much sodium. That excess sodium won't put any permanent pounds on you, but you may feel puffy and swollen for a few days afterward, which won't do much for your morale if you happen to have a fitting.

The recommendations that follow will help you make the most of your meals on the run.

BREAKFAST

If you're ordering at a drive-up window, beware of the seemingly benign but secretly villainous breakfast sandwich—that is, eggs and cheese plus ham, bacon, or sausage on a biscuit or croissant. These sandwiches range from 400 to 800 calories and pack half a day's fat allowance. It's hard to believe that something as light and fluffy as a croissant can be fattening, but it can carry up to 25 more grams of fat than an English muffin; a biscuit is no lightweight, either, being chockful of 17 more grams of fat than an English muffin. So opt for that English muffin and an order of scrambled eggs or a single box of cereal with low-fat milk.

Another seemingly innocent breakfast splurge is a bagel with cream cheese or butter. The average bagel now weighs in at 4 ounces and has 320 calories before the schmear, which adds another 100 to 200 calories of pure fat. Right behind the bagel is the jumbo muffin. The typical raisin bran, corn, or apple-cinnamon variety from the corner cafe can pack up to 500 calories with 25 grams of fat. You're better off getting a fruit smoothie and two slices of raisin bread topped with jam. Or go for a low-fat granola bar, a container of yogurt, and a banana for 300 calories and 3 grams of fat.

Eating between Fittings

FOOD COURT IN THE MALL

Approach this area just like you would a buffet (see the tips on this in Chapter Seven). You've got to see what your choices are and avoid the hype of "combo specials" and "super-sized meal deals." You may get your best calorie-conscious deal by buying part of your meal at one counter and the rest at another.

The biggest source of calories in the food court is usually the meat, whether it's a beef patty, hot dog, or piece of fried chicken. You're better off skipping the meat and finding a vegetable meal you can enjoy; get your protein at another time and place where you can have better quality control.

A large baked potato will have about 300 calories, no fat, and only 25 mg. of sodium, but watch out for those weighty toppings like cheese and bacon bits. Your best bets for toppings are plain broccoli and a packet of sour cream for a total of 75 calories, 6 grams of fat, and 15 mg. sodium.

At the Chinese food stand, one cup of broccoli and bean curd with a cup of plain white rice will provide about 350 calories with 5 grams of fat and 100 mgs. of sodium if you don't add any additional soy sauce. Chicken chow mein is also a reasonable choice at 255 calories and 10 grams of fat per cup, but the sodium can go over 500 mg.

If there is a concession selling big specialty salads, it is worth checking out. What you want is lots of garden-variety vegetables with plain tuna or chicken on top and a low-fat or nonfat salad dressing. Skip the pasta, cheeses, and olives.

Another great option is a couple of sushi rolls at about 150 calories each, no fat, and less than 100 mg. of sodium. Be cautious about dipping sauces, however.

Tips for other concessions in the food court and for all those freestanding fast-food places in other locations:

FAST-FOOD BURGERS

Your best bet here is the kiddie burger with its small dollops of ketchup and mustard. Cheese can add another 100 calories and 8 grams of fat, so try to avoid it. Find some kind of side salad to go with your burger instead of the fries. Even a small fat-free frozen yogurt is a wiser choice than the fries.

Forget the deluxe burgers with "double anything" and special sauces or extra toppings like bacon and cheese. These are not good foods for brides or for anyone else who is going to be trying on a custom-fitted dress in the near future.

CHICKEN

The key words here are *roasted* or *grilled*, not fried. Beyond that, avoid the skin, pay extra for white meat if you must, and cancel the secret sauce on a chicken sandwich.

PIZZA

The pizza shop has more potential than most people realize. A single slice of cheese pizza with a thin crust has about 275 calories and 5 grams of fat. It's the second or third slice that can get you into trouble. Ask for a side order of vegetable toppings or a cup of minestrone soup to keep you from reaching for those additional slices. And, of course, steer clear of meat toppings, double crust, cheese-in-the-crust, and deep-dish features.

SUBS AND SANDWICHES

Some of the chains are making it easier to order sensibly because they've added lower-calorie and lower-fat sandwiches. If no such specially labeled menu items are available, go for the turkey breast; next best, roast beef; third best, boiled ham. If you can pass up the cheese, you'll save 100 calories per slice. Same goes for the mayonnaise, at 100 calories per tablespoon. Ask for whole-wheat or whole-grain bread, and feel free to pile on the shredded lettuce, sliced tomato, onions, roasted peppers, and any other vegetables on hand.

Proceed with caution at the sight of tortilla "wraps" and "stuffed" pitas. Most contain more high-fat dressing and cheese than you might realize, and those wraps and pitas are much higher in calories than two slices of bread.

MEXICAN

This menu can be a real challenge since the dishes have so many components. There's the shell, soft or crisp, the meat or bean filling, then cheese and several toppings. On its own, each of these ingredients can produce very big numbers in the calorie and fat columns. When put all together, the result can be disastrous.

Look for anything on the menu listed as "light." If there are no lighter choices, make due with a chicken taco with extra salsa but no sour cream, and a side order of Mexican rice. A cup of gazpacho and a quesadilla will do the trick, as well.

POPULAR RESTAURANT CHAINS

Once you're looking at a printed menu instead of a lighted menu board, your choices will undoubtedly be better. Scan every section for foods you can put together to make a meal. A combination of appetizers and side dishes may do the job instead of an entree. It is also a good idea to look for any healthy heart symbols or spa cuisine designations among the menu choices.

An important way you'll save calories is to order a la carte. As economical as the early-bird special and complete meal prices may seem, they are costing you more calories than you can afford right now. Find out what you want and order only that. Many a dish of rice pudding with whipped cream has been eaten just because it was included with the dinner.

Don't expect too much help in the way of substitutions or special preparation in these chain restaurants. The menus are almost always inflexible—save, say, allowing you to substitute sliced tomatoes for the hash browns, as one of us did recently at Denny's. Count on having to ask a lot of questions about how things are served and on scraping off the sauces and coatings you don't want to eat.

GROCERY STORE/DELI TAKEOUT

A real advantage here is that you pay for most items by weight. You can actually order three ounces of turkey breast and a quarter of a pound of coleslaw and get just that. You can also buy a single banana, an eight-ounce carton of cottage cheese, and a small can of low-salt tomato juice if you want.

The prepared hot foods in these places are generally not diet-friendly. But the rotisserie chicken is (you can remove the skin for further calorie and fat savings), along with the fresh vegetables and fruit salads. Single-serving portions of condiments like low-fat mayonnaise and salad dressing are helpful, too.

You can have a sandwich made to order on the whole-grain bread or roll of your choice and have it piled high with roasted peppers, sliced mushrooms, and bean sprouts if the spirit moves you. It's all there for the asking.

Stroll down the aisles for a box of low-fat granola bars or a bag of unsalted pretzels to munch on later in the day, if needed. Then pick up a pack of gum or a roll of mints in the checkout line to pop in your mouth after one granola bar so that you won't eat the whole box!

CONVENIENCE STORES

These can be a challenge if you never go past the most convenient, ready-to-eat items on display at the front of the store. You *do* have other options. Just past the grilling hot dogs and nachos you'll find a freezer case. Look for a healthy-style frozen entree and pop it in the store's microwave for a quick lunch.

Get past the shelves stocked with chips, dips, and pork rinds and you'll find other shelves stocked with canned goods you can use, like tuna in water, applesauce, and vegetarian baked beans. There are also boxes of cereal, raisins, and graham crackers—all low in fat. Then stroll by the refrigerated cases for string cheese, yogurt, and hard-boiled eggs.

Right around the corner from the candy bars you'll find popcorn and fruit-filled cereal bars. Just keep your eyes open and don't be impulsive. Since nearly every food in the store has a label on it, read the nutrition facts before making any decision, and you'll be fine.

SALAD BARS

A salad bar may seem like a no-brainer place to get a safe meal, but there are some fat traps even in this glorified setting. Walk past anything covered in mayonnaise, like potato or macaroni salad and tuna, ham, or egg salad. You also don't want to linger too long in front of the crispy Chinese noodles, seasoned croutons, and sunflower seeds.

Focus on all things from Mother Nature's garden: mixed greens, shredded carrots and cabbage, sliced cucumbers and radishes, pepper strips or rings, raw onion rings, and broccoli florets. Garnish with a light sprinkling of grated cheese or cubed ham or sea legs (imitation crab and lobster pieces made from processed seasoned whitefish).

Then, to top it all off, take advantage of the low-calorie dressing or your own vinaigrette with lots of balsamic vinegar and a splash of olive oil.

Okay, now you know what to eat when you're out and about on your own. But, as your wedding grows ever closer, what do you do when well-meaning friends, relatives, and coworkers lure you to calorie-laden celebrations in your honor? You don't want to be rude. You don't want to be ungrateful. You don't want to spoil anyone's fun. But you don't want a bigger butt, either. Read on!

CHAPTER SEVEN

S H O W E R E D   W I T H   C A L O R I E S

s if you didn't have enough "on your plate" right now, getting the right addresses on the invitations, selecting gifts for your attendants, deciding what color linens you want in the bathroom of your new apartment, *and* trying to lose weight, your family and friends will heap on more. In the final month before your wedding, you'll be feted at successive parties with coworkers, girlfriends, bridesmaids, and extended family where you must be the gracious guest of honor. The date, time, and place of each event will often be out of your control, and the menu preset.

These situations can spell diet disaster if you don't have a game plan at the ready to bail you out. Here's what you need to know.

Rule #1: It is easier to control your surroundings than to control your behavior.

- When possible, position yourself as far from the food as you can. If you are sitting in front of a table laden with chips and dips, salted nuts, or chocolate cordials, you can't be expected to ignore them. If they are across the room, you won't be as likely to eat them.

- Suggest a restaurant that you know has a "safe" menu when eating out or on the run. It's impossible to eat sensibly when your only choice is a burger and fries.

- Stay out of the kitchen, lunchroom, vending lounge, and other food traps when stressed out, overtired, or otherwise out of sorts. You will use food to medicate your emotions if it's nearby, so don't go near it.

Rule #2: Know what you are eating before you put anything in your mouth.

- Look up serving size and caloric information first, and then decide if you can afford to eat the food. It is too late to substitute a ham and Swiss on rye for the Monte Cristo after you have swallowed the last bite of the batter-dipped and pan-fried sandwich.

- Ask questions about menu items and make your

preferences clear before placing your order. Marinated vegetables can be swimming in olive oil or in balsamic vinegar. The difference is crucial to your calorie count.

Rule #3: Record everything you eat immediately after you eat it.

• With so much going on in your life, don't expect your short-term memory to be as sharp as it was in your carefree, pre-engagement days. The side dish of coleslaw or croutons on a salad can add another hundred calories to a meal. Keep a small notepad in your purse or grab a cocktail napkin off the table and jot down exactly what and how much you ate before leaving the restaurant or party.

In all of the charts in this chapter, we provide the *average* calorie value of each food item since there may be many versions of the food. The serving sizes are typical, but your actual portion size may vary.

Use these additional suggestions when attending specific functions in your honor:

LUNCHEON WITH COWORKERS

• Call home and cancel any dinner plans you might have had. You don't need two big meals in one day. Have a nice salad or bowl of vegetable soup that night.

Luncheon with Coworkers

Diet Disasters	cals/serving	Diet Dreams	cals/serving
Regular beer	150/12 oz.	Light beer	100/12 oz.
Rum and Coke	200/8 oz.	Diet Coke	1/12 oz.
Wine spritzer	100/12 oz.	Seltzer with lime	0
Nacho platter	350/6 to 8 pcs.	California roll	120/6-in. roll
Buffalo chicken wings	450/4 pcs.	Humus and pita triangles	150/ 1/4 cup humus plus
Potato skins	300/4 pcs.		4 triangles
		Steamed artichoke	60 each
New England clam chowder	165/cup	Manhattan clam chowder	75/cup
Cream of tomato	160/cup	Gazpacho	60/cup
Vegetable beef soup	175/cup	Minestrone	85/cup
Tuna salad sandwich	500/avg.	Bacon, lettuce, and tomato	350
Hamburger on bun	500/avg.	Garden burger on bun	275
Chef salad w/ Russian dressing	600	Spinach salad w/ vinaigrette	350
Peach pie	350/slice	Peach crisp	200 per 3/4 cup
Carrot cake with cream cheese frosting	475/slice	Pound cake	200 per 1-in. slice
Chocolate brownie	250 per 2x2x1-in. piece	Chocolate biscotti	100/oz. or 5x1-in. piece

Showered with Calories

- If given a choice of where to go for the luncheon, suggest a diet-friendly place, like a Thai, Japanese, or Middle Eastern restaurant.
- Opt for seltzer with lime or a fruit juice spritzer instead of an alcoholic beverage to help keep your wits about you when the ordering begins.
- Check the appetizer menu for possible lunch options, like a seafood cocktail and grilled vegetables.
- Pose for a picture with each of your friends around the table so you're less likely to nibble on the shared nacho platter and chicken wings.
- If you receive cards and gifts, start to open them when the food is served, and be sure to read each card out loud. You'll be too busy to do much eating.
- Definitely share dessert, then don't eat your share.

NIGHT OUT WITH THE GIRLS

- Spend that afternoon in your bathing suit to fortify your willpower not to indulge.
- Wear something clingy, fitted, or belted for a constant reminder not to overeat.
- Give yourself a curfew so you aren't tempted to barhop and prolong the drinking and eating all night.
- Order an iced fat-free latte—it'll look like you're drinking a Black Russian, but with far fewer calories.

Night Out with the Girls

Diet Disasters	cals/serving	Diet Dreams	cals/serving
Black Russian	275/8 oz.	Fat-free latte	40/8 oz.
Gin and tonic	175/8 oz.	Scotch and soda	100/8 oz.
Piña colada	370/8 oz.	Screwdriver	175/8 oz.
Guacamole and chips	250/ 1/4 cup dip and 1 oz. chips	Salsa and chips	160/ 1/4 cup dip, and 1 oz. chips
Fried eggplant	250/cup	Roasted veggies	100/cup
Egg roll	180/ea.	Wonton soup	80/cup
Beef and bean enchilada	400/ea.	Beef fajitas	250/ea.
Veal Parmesan	600/serving	Veal Marsala	400/serving
Chicken lo mein	400/cup	Chicken chow mein	250/cup
Refried beans	250/cup	Black bean soup	125/cup
Fried mozzarella sticks	450/5 pcs.	Sliced mozzarella and tomato	200/2 oz. cheese, 1/2 tomato plus vinaigrette
Fried rice	375/cup	White rice	160/cup
Ice cream	400/cup	Sorbet	200/cup
Cheesecake	450/slice	Zabaglione	160/svg.
Almond cookie	45 ea.	Fortune cookie	25 ea.

- Avoid noshing at the bar on salty snacks. They make you thirsty and you'll end up drinking even more.
- If you do end up toasting your own health along with the girls, order a nonalcoholic drink in between each full-proof one to dilute the damage.
- When it's time to order, suggest you share appetizers around the table, then simply skip your turn after one or two samples when the plates come your way.
- Do not ask for a doggy bag unless you really have a dog and really plan on giving the rest of that pasta to him or her. You don't need it.

THE SURPRISE BRIDAL SHOWER

- Slip into the kitchen and pour yourself a big glass of water after the initial glare of flashbulbs and tears of surprise have passed. Drink the entire thing to help fill yourself up before you reenter the party.
- Mingle, socialize, and greet all your long-lost friends and relatives. It will keep you talking rather than eating.
- Put some munchies on a party napkin or small plate and limit yourself to eating only those. Don't eat any hors d'oeuvres directly from the serving tray and platters—it's too hard to keep track of how much you've had.

- This is a good time to opt for a "virgin" drink like plain tomato juice or orange juice with a twist.
- Don't let your well-meaning hostess "fix a plate" for you. Get on line with everyone else and make your own selections from the chafing dishes.
- Practice saying "thank you" when given a gift and "no thank you" when offered another dessert.
- Decline the offer to take home the other half of the shower cake or the remains of Aunt Bessie's macaroni salad. Say that your refrigerator is broken and you have nowhere to store it.

The Surprise Bridal Shower

Menu Items	Calories/Serving
Party punch	200/cup
Mixed nuts	200/1/4 cup
Spinach dip and bread	100/1/4 cup dip, 4 bread cubes
Finger sandwiches	100 each
Deviled eggs	75/half egg
Tossed salad w/ Italian dressing	50/cup
Baked ziti	300/cup
Sheet cake	150/2×2-in. square
Petits fours	85 each

TASTING NIGHT AT THE CATERER'S

- Scrutinize the full menu in advance and circle those items that you must make a decision about to avoid eating things you weren't planning to serve anyway.
- Sample each item as if you were a food critic—get the essence of the taste and texture in the first bite.
- Take as many people along as you are permitted and let them cast their votes on the food so you don't have to try everything.
- Be the stenographer, keeping track of what was served and what the comments were. You'll be too busy to overeat.
- Don't sample anything that is not dependent on the chef's culinary skills, such as the salad, assorted cheeses and crackers, raw shellfish, baked potato, melon balls, etc.
- Dip the tines of a fork into any dressings or dips you wish to taste.
- Step into the ladies' room midway through the evening and run cold water over your wrists to revive your numbed senses after an hour of sampling.

THE REHEARSAL DINNER

- Try on your honeymoon outfit that afternoon as a reminder of how great you look after all of your hard work.

The Rehearsal Dinner

Menu Items	Calories/Serving
Red or white wine	100/4 oz.
French onion soup w/ melted cheese and bread	30/cup + 150
French bread w/ butter	50/2-oz. slice + 35/teaspoon
Mesclun salad w/ French dressing	10/cup + 50/tablespoon
Broiled flounder stuffed with crab meat	200/6 oz. + 150/cup
Boiled new potatoes roasted in olive oil	100/3 potatoes + 100
Asparagus w/ hollandaise sauce	25/6 spears 50/2 tablespoons
Crème brûlée	+ 200/ 1/2 cup

- Be sure to eat before going to the rehearsal since it often takes longer than anyone planned and you don't want to arrive at the restaurant starving.
- Limit yourself to one alcoholic drink to toast the occasion—preferably *with* your meal, not before.
- Order something you like, but not a favorite dish. You'll be less inclined to gobble up every bite.
- Be sure to sit next to your fiancé and pass off any unwanted food onto his plate.

- When prodded to order an appetizer or to eat more food than you want to, refuse by confessing that you are really nervous and feel like bumble bees are buzzing around inside your stomach.
- To shave calories, avoid "add ons" in the form of sauces, spreads, dressings, stuffings, and toppings.
- Watch out for high-salt items like soups, tomato sauce, barbecue sauce, ham, and anything with soy sauce on it. You can't afford to be bloated this close to the wedding.

NAVIGATING A BUFFET LINE

- Walk up, down, and around all of the serving tables, including the dessert stand, to see what is being served. Then predetermine exactly what you're going to eat from the available choices.
- If something looks fabulous but fattening, go ahead and have a small portion, but don't waste any calories on foods you can get any time, such as rice pilaf, potato salad, or Jell-O.
- If there isn't an "undressed" salad, make one for yourself out of the garnishes. Look for things like pepper rings, cherry tomatoes, kale, radish roses, parsley, and orange slices.
- Eat in courses, just as if you were dining a la carte, and sit down to eat each course before returning to the line for more. With any luck, the line will be too long to bother get-

ting up again, or the food will run out and you won't be able to eat as much.

- Use a salad or dessert plate for your selections and you'll *have* to take smaller portions.

- Choose a table as far from the buffet as possible to make the trip back more difficult.

- Don't let anyone else bring you any food while he or she is at the buffet.

- Do not eat anything off your plate while moving through the line, not even a stray cheese cube.

- Visit the ladies' room after your plate is cleared and brush your teeth or rinse your mouth with mouthwash to diminish the desire for dessert. Almost everything tastes awful when you have "minty mouth."

- Never weigh yourself the day after a meal like this—it will only weaken your resolve. Most buffet and banquet foods are covered with salty sauces to keep them from drying out. You will undoubtedly retain fluid for a few days after eating them, which will show up on your scale as water weight—but it will pass.

THE WEDDING DAY MENU

- Eat *slowly*, and signal the waiter to clear your plates before you've finished.

The Wedding Dinner

Menu Items	Calories/Serving
Champagne	80/4 oz.
APPETIZERS	
Stuffed mushroom	50 ea.
Mini quiche	75 ea.
Cheese puff	100 ea.
Spinach wrapped in phyllo dough	125 ea.
Cocktail frank wrapped in baked dough	150 ea.
FIRST COURSES	
Caesar salad	100/cup
Fresh fruit cocktail w/sherbet	150
Cream of mushroom soup	60/cup
MAIN COURSE ENTREES	
Lobster tail	150/6 oz.
Grilled salmon	300/6 oz.
Chicken cordon bleu	450/serving
Prime rib	800/8 oz.
SIDE STARCHES	
Wild rice pilaf	120/ 1/2 cup
Cloverleaf roll w/ butter	150 ea.
Bread stuffing	180/ 1/2 cup
Twice-baked stuffed potato	275/serving
Fettuccini Alfredo	300/cup

The Wedding Dinner (cont.)

Menu Items	Calories/Serving
SIDE VEGETABLES	
Glazed carrots	50/ 1/2 cup
Green beans w/almonds and butter sauce	80/ 1/2 cup
Peas w/ mushrooms and cream sauce	100/cup
DESSERTS	
Coffee w/ cream and sugar	30/cup
Chocolate-covered strawberry	60 ea.
Two-layer cake with buttercream	300/1-in. slice
APERITIF Crème de menthe	185/ 1-1/2 oz.

- Stay hydrated with water—it's a long day of dancing and posing and lugging around that gown.

POST-RECEPTION ROOM SERVICE IN
THE BRIDAL SUITE

- Tantalize one another with blissfully low-calorie foods of love, such as peeled, seedless grapes, oysters on the half shell, fresh raspberries, and caviar on toast points.

Showered with Calories

Room Service!

Menu Items	Calories/Serving
Raw oysters	50/med.
Caviar	40/tablespoon
Toast points	20/ea. triangle
Seedless grapes	80/cup or 20 pieces
Raspberries	60/cup
Camembert	85/oz.
Brie	95/oz.
Townhouse crackers	30/2 pieces
Hershey's Kisses or Hugs	26 per piece
Aerosol whipped cream	200 per cup!

- Put on your sexiest, skimpiest negligee and you won't even think about eating.

CHAPTER EIGHT

SETTING UP A SLIM KITCHEN

*I*s your kitchen cooperating? Is it adapting to your new healthy eating habits? If not, put it on a diet. Don't let it tempt you with that half-bag of mini M&M's you ostensibly keep for baking. Don't let it beckon you to the freezer for that pan full of cheese-engorged lasagna. Throw that stuff out. Do a kitchen "remodel"—not just to make your life easier while you're dieting, but to help you maintain your weight loss and your healthy eating style once you weigh what you want to. Let us count the simple and (mostly) inexpensive ways.

SLIM-CONSCIOUS COOKWARE
AND GADGETS

If you can't afford these items right now, why not list some of them on your bridal registry?

Bamboo steamers: They look like brimless bamboo hats. Use them on top of a pot of boiling water to steam vegetables and other foods; cooking oil isn't necessary. Steaming retains nutrients that are often lost during conventional cooking. The steamers come in various sizes to accommodate different pots, and they're interesting-looking enough that you can hang them on the wall, if they fit in with your kitchen decor or storage space is a problem.

Crock pot or pressure cooker: Both allow you to cook meat and/or vegetables without losing nutrients and in liquid instead of oil. *See* For Your Cookbook Shelf in this chapter for a great book about this style of cooking.

Extra ice cube trays: Use them to freeze stock, egg whites, fruit purees, sauces, etc.

Fat separator: Usually in the form of a measuring cup, this nifty gadget makes the fat from the juices of meat or poultry float to the top. Open a valve on the bottom to release the fat-free juices, then use the juices to moisturize and flavor the cooked meat. Many models will also allow you to separate egg whites from yolks, a requirement in many low-fat recipes.

Food processors: These will save you a lot of time as you add more fruits and veggies to your diet. Larger models (which hold about eleven cups) are great for chopping and slicing. "Mini-prep" processors (about two and a half cups) are just right for tackling small but time-consuming tasks like chopping herbs and garlic and grating cheese.

Garlic press: Another way to make the most of this pungent, tasty, healthy bulb. One we like—sold by the Williams Sonoma chain—has a stainless-steel press screen that pivots out for easy cleaning and a comfortable, ergonomic plastic handle.

Kitchen sprouter: All you need are some seeds, a little water, and a few days to grow sprouts in your kitchen for your salads and vegetable dishes.

Nonstick pans and bakeware: Going nonstick is one of the most dramatic ways to cut your fat intake. Consider that when you cook with a conventional pan, you must use several table-spoons of oil or other fat, while with a nonstick pan a tea-spoon—or a single pass of a nonstick cooking spray—will suffice. The average tablespoon of cooking oil (and remember, you may need several) has about 14 grams of fat and 122 calories. When you cut back to a teaspoon, each of those numbers is reduced by two-thirds. A general rule when buying nonstick cookware: Opt for the heaviest you can afford.

Oil sprayer: Fill this device with olive oil or another oil and it does double duty—you can use it to lightly coat your pots and pans before cooking, or you can spray the oil directly on salads and vegetables. In either case, spraying instead of pouring saves you fat and calories. One we particularly like: the Misto olive oil sprayer.

Rice cooker: Rice is a staple of a low-fat lifestyle, but even experienced cooks complain about not being able to cook it quite right. That's the beauty of a rice cooker, which monitors the steam heat to produce fluffy, evenly cooked, perfectly done rice. Most models have a keep-warm or warm-up feature. You can steam other foods in this appliance, as well.

Salad spinner: With this handy item, you wash and place lettuce or other vegetables inside a strainer that fits into a plastic bowl. Then you either pull a cord or pump a button to set the strainer spinning. The result: fresh, crisp lettuce and veggies.

Steamer basket: This inexpensive metal gadget has hinged, petal-like sides that will adjust so that you can convert almost any pot or pan into a steamer. As with bamboo and other forms of steamers, this type will keep nutrients and flavors from escaping from vegetables.

Stove-top grill: A low-fat method of cooking that will give you the taste of barbecue even in the depths of winter. Its nonstick cooking surface requires little or no cooking oil, making cleanup, as they say, a snap. Many models can be used on either gas or electric stove tops.

Wok: The deep, flared sides of this type of cookware give you a maximum amount of surface area to stir, toss, and cook foods evenly, efficiently, and very quickly. You can even stir fry with water or broth, instead of oil, with little detectable change in taste.

Yogurt strainer: Here's a mesh gadget that will strain the fluid out of yogurt so that it's creamier and spreadable.

STOCKING THE PANTRY

Low-fat and low-calorie don't have to mean low taste. Seasoning is the key. One of the biggest threats to calorie-controlled eating is "menu monotony." If you have to eat chicken five nights a week, you better learn ways to make it taste new and delicious every time or you'll be foraging around for some peanut butter on crackers with chocolate morsels on top an hour after dinner. Use spices to keep the taste alive. Many low-fat recipes will call for one or more of the ingredients below. In fact, most of the major spice companies themselves offer Websites brimming with such recipes. Just type your seasoning brand name—such as McCormick Spices or Durkee Spices—into your favorite search engine. You'll also often find offers of free recipe books and pamphlets on the spice bottles. We've got lots more tips on using spices in Chapter Ten on page 209.

No one expects you to run out and buy *everything* on the following lists; you can just pick things up as you need them. Nevertheless, our ideal healthy kitchen would be stocked with the following:

Dry Seasonings: allspice, basil, bay leaves, butter-flavored sprinkles, caraway, cayenne pepper, celery flakes or seeds, chili powder, cinnamon, cloves, coriander, cream of tartar, cumin, curry, dill, garlic (powder or minced), ginger, marjoram, mustard powder, nutmeg, onion (powder or minced), oregano, paprika, parsley flakes, pepper (regular), pepper (coarse-ground), red pepper flakes, rosemary, sage, tarragon, thyme, and turmeric.

Wet Seasonings, Oils, Condiments, and Cooking Liquids:
applesauce (unsweetened), chicken broth (fat-free), chutney,
cooking spray (nonstick), duck sauce, flavor sprays (olive oil
or garlic), flavored extracts (vanilla to start), hot pepper
sauce, jams, marmalade, preserves, ketchup, lemon juice
(bottled), lime juice (bottled), liquid smoke, marinades (nonfat), mayonnaise (reduced fat), mustards (Dijon; coarse
country-style), oils in bottles (canola, olive, and one nut oil—
e.g. peanut, walnut, or sesame), salad dressings (light, oil-
free, and/or fat-free), salsa and picante sauce, soy sauce
(light), teriyaki sauce, vinegars (flavored, such as red and
white wine, apple cider, balsamic), wine for cooking (one dry
red, one dry white, one sherry), and Worcestershire sauce.

Staples—Dry, Canned, Bottled: artichoke hearts (packed
in water), baby cocktail corn (canned), beans (canned,
assorted varieties), bread (whole-wheat or whole-grain),
boxed grains—rices (such as brown, wild, basmati, arborio;
couscous, barley, wheat pilaf), evaporated skim milk, fruit
(canned, in its own juice), green chili peppers (chopped),
hearts of palm (jar or can), honey, molasses, mushrooms
(dried or canned), pastas (dry, in the styles you prefer), pita
bread (whole-wheat), snacks (low-fat, such as pretzels,
baked tortilla chips, rice cakes, and nonfat rye and whole-
grain crackers), sweet red peppers (roasted, whole, and/or
chopped), syrup (light, maple-flavored), tomato paste, toma-

to sauce, tomatoes (whole, canned; regular or Italian-style), tomatoes (chopped up and flavored, such as with garlic and herbs), tortillas (corn or whole-wheat), tuna (packed in water), water chestnuts (canned), and wheat germ—a great substitute for bread crumbs!

FOR YOUR COOKBOOK SHELF

No low-fat, low-calorie kitchen is complete without at least a handful of good cookbooks. If you love to browse the cooking section at your local bookstore, keep these tips in mind before plunking down your money:

- If you're not an experienced cook, make sure the cookbook you buy has lots of pictures and/or illustrations.
- Look for books in which each recipe has a nutrient analysis—that is, a breakdown of the calories, fat grams, carbohydrates, etc., per serving.
- If the goal of getting everything done at the same time—entrees, side dishes, salads, etc.—scares you, search for a book with menu plans, such as "While the chicken simmers, wash and cut up the vegetables. . . ."
- Check the copyright date of the book. You want a book that's new enough so that the nutritional information and the ingredients needed are up to date.

Coming up: Our recommendations for cookbooks with healthy recipes; we've thrown in a few fitness books and calorie counters, as well. Prices listed are full retail; you may be able to get substantial discounts if you shop around.

If anybody asks you for shower or wedding gift ideas, why not share this section? Or . . . register at a bookstore. Or . . . suggest a bookstore gift certificate.

ALL-PURPOSE

Complete Book of Low-Fat Cooking (Low-Fat Cookbook Series) by Sunset Books, 1996, $29.95. At 432 pages, this book features more than 500 innovative low-fat versions of classic dishes.

The New Joy of Cooking by Irma S. Rombauer, et al; Scribner, 1997, $30. The newest edition of this culinary bible features thousands of traditional and up-to-date recipes reflecting the tastes of the new millennium.

1,000 Low-Fat Recipes by Terry Blonder Golson; Macmillan, 1998, $29.95. Crammed not only with recipes for low-fat soups, salads, appetizers, and sandwiches, but with nutrition guidelines, an ingredient glossary, menu-planning techniques, and more.

1,001 Low Fat Recipes: Quick, Easy, Great-Tasting Recipes for Your Whole Family by Sue Spitler and Linda R. Yoakam; Surrey

Books, 1995, $19.95. Weighing in at 660 pages, this is a wonderful book for neophytes because you can see at a glance how much time each dish requires. Everything's covered—appetizers, snacks, sauces, pasta, side dishes, salads, soups, entrees, seafood, pizza, and desserts, all from a variety of cuisines.

INSTRUCTIONAL

Cooking Light's Low-Fat Ways to Lose Weight by Susan McIntosh; Oxmoor House, 1996, $18.95. Seven days' worth of low-fat menus, ideas for quick breakfasts, lunches, and snacks plus healthy substitutions and terrific recipes.

The Essential Cookbook: From Market to Table, Everything You Need to Know About Selecting, Preparing, Cooking, and Serving the Very Best Foods by Caroline Conran, Terrence Conran, and Simon Hopkinson; Stewart, Tabori & Chang, 1997, $50. Not just a recipe book, but an encyclopedia! Learn about various cooking techniques and equipment—from the measuring cup to the blow torch. More than 450 recipes, sumptuously photographed.

The Good Housekeeping Step-by-Step Cookbook edited by Susan Westmoreland; Hearst Books, 1997, $30. More than 1,000 mostly mainstream recipes, 1,800 photos, and step-by-step instructions that include estimates for both prep and cooking times.

How to Cook Everything: Simple Recipes for Great Food by Mark Bittman; Macmillan, 1998, $25. The author contributes the Minimalist column to the Dining section of the *New York Times*. This is a 1,500-recipe multicultural feast, and that includes American classics.

Prevention's the Healthy Cook: The Ultimate Illustrated Kitchen Guide to Great Low-Fat Food by Matthew Hoffman and David Joachim; Rodale Press, 1997, $27.95. The basics of healthy cooking without the frou-frou. Numerous charts and illustrations demonstrate such things as the differences between cooking utensils. More than 1,000 healthy recipes, contributed by such food gods as Jacques Pepin.

GENERAL NUTRITION, DIETING, AND FITNESS

The American Dietetic Association's Complete Food and Nutrition Guide by Roberta Larson Duyff; Chronimed, 1998, $24.95. How to combine good taste and good health in every meal and snack.

Dieting for Dummies by Jane Kirby, the American Dietetic Association; IDG Books, 1998, $19.99. Basic, reliable facts about all facets of weight loss, including information about eating disorders, overweight kids, dietary guidelines, fat substitutes, calorie-shaving tips, a comparison of weight-loss programs, and an exposé of diet fads and scams.

Fitting in Fitness: Hundreds of Simple Ways to Put More Physical Activity into Your Life by the American Heart Association; HarperCollins, 1997, $4.99. Easy to read, and includes hundreds of creative ways to increase activity at home, at work, and on the road. Ideas for kids, too.

QUICK AND EASY

Healthy Cooking for People Who Don't Have Time to Cook by Jeanne Jones; Rodale Press, 1999, $15.95. Written by the author of the "Cook It Light" newspaper column, many of the recipes can be prepared within fifteen minutes and require only fresh vegetables, meat, pantry staples, and/or spices. All are low-calorie and low-fat.

Quick & Healthy Recipes and Ideas (Vol. II) by Brenda Ponichtera; ScaleDown Publishing, 1995, $16.95. Easy and healthful recipes, menu ideas, and tips.

20 Minutes to Dinner: Quick, Low-Fat, Low-Calorie Vegetarian Meals by Bryanna Clark Grogan; The Book Publishing Co., 1997, $12.95. Tasty, nutritious dishes based on the Mediterranean/Asian model of eating—plenty of grains, fruits, and vegetables.

SPECIAL DIETARY NEEDS

Kosher Light: Your Traditional Jewish Favorites Cooked Healthy by Zillah Bahar; Penguin Studio, 1998, $17.95. Easy-to-prepare, strictly kosher recipes.

365 Healthful Ways to Cook Tofu and Other Meat Alternatives by Robin Robertson; Plume/Dutton Signet, 1996, $15.95. How to use tofu in mainstream dishes with familiar sauces and flavors. Also includes recipes centering around grains and vegetables.

20 Minutes to Dinner: Quick, Low-Fat, Low-Calorie Vegetarian Meals. See description above under Quick and Easy section.

Vegetarian Cooking for Everyone by Deborah Madison; Broadway Books, 1997, $40. A comprehensive cookbook that features some recipes for vegans and all for vegetarians. They can also be served with meat, fish, and poultry.

JUST FOR TWO

Healthy Cooking for 2 (Or Just You): Low-Fat Recipes with Half the Fuss and Double the Taste by Frances Price; Rodale Press, 1997, $15.95. Fresh ideas, practical tips, and delicious recipes for singles, couples, and small families.

Light Cooking for Two by Anne C. Chappell and Deborah Garrison Lowery; Oxmoor House, 1995, $29.95. More than 200 pages of recipes that can also be easily converted to single servings.

ETHNIC/REGIONAL CUISINES

Down Home Wholesome: 300 Low-Fat Recipes from a New Soul Kitchen by Danella Carter; Penguin USA, 1998, $15.95. Healthy alterations to classic soul dishes.

Healthy Mediterranean Cooking by Rena Salaman; Stewart Tabori & Chang, 1996, $29.95. Low in cholesterol and saturated fats and brimming with the healthiest of ingredients, these recipes come from the well-loved cuisines of France, Italy, Spain, and Greece.

Healthy Mexican Cooking by Velda de la Garza; Appletree Press, 1995, $15.95. Authentic, low-fat Mexican recipes.

Vegetarian Times Low-Fat & Fast Asian: 150 Easy Meatless Recipes by the editors of *Vegetarian Times* magazine; Macmillan, 1997, $16. Covers everything from stir-fries to noodle dishes to Thai food and sushi.

FISH AND POULTRY

Light Ways with Poultry by the food editors of *PREVEN-TION* magazine; Rodale Press, 1995, $15.95. Includes make-ahead sauces and gravies, special cooking techniques, and quick and tasty low-fat recipes.

Low-Fat Ways to Cook Fish and Shellfish by Susan McIntosh; Leisure Arts, 1997, $18.95. Reader-friendly book featuring preparation, cooking techniques, and recipes for lobster, crab claws, and clams.

PASTA

Cook It Light: Pasta, Rice, and Beans by Jeanne Jones; Macmillan, 1998, $14.95. Written by the author of the popular "Cook It Light" newspaper column, this book contains more than 200 recipes and offers good advice on cooking techniques.

500 (Practically) Fat-Free Pasta Recipes by Sarah Schlesinger; Villard Books, 1997, $25. This author concerns herself not just with fat content, but with calories, as well.

366 Delicious Ways to Cook Pasta with Vegetables by Dolores Riccio; Plume, 1997, $16.95. Organized alphabetically by vegetable, from artichoke to zucchini.

SALADS/VEGETABLES

Low-Fat Ways to Cook Salads and Side Dishes by Susan McIntosh; Oxmoor House, 1999, $18.95. Besides its more than 175 recipes, this book is rich with buying, storing, and cooking methods.

100 Low-Fat Small Meal and Salad Recipes (The Complete Book of Food Counts Cookbook Series) by Corinne T. Netzer; Dell Books, 1998, $5.99. Recipes not just for salads but for soups and sandwiches, as well.

100 Low-Fat Vegetable and Legume Recipes (The Complete Book of Food Counts Cookbook Series) by Corinne T. Netzer; Dell Books, 1998, $5.99. Vegetarian main courses plus soups and salads.

GRILLING

All Fired Up! Outdoor and Indoor Grilling by John Howard and Margaret Howard; Firefly Books, 1998, $24.95. More than 150 recipes for meats, poultry, fish, veggies, and fruits and the different methods of grilling them, such as direct, spit-roasting, and kebabs.

Grilling for Dummies by Marie Rama and John F. Mariana; IDG Books, 1998, $19.95. Part reference, part cookbook, part cooking class, with 130 recipes.

PRESSURE COOKING

The Pressured Cook by Lorna Sass; William Morrow, 1999, $19.95. More than 75 recipes that are full of natural ingredients, low in fat, and ready to eat in less than an hour.

BAKING AND DESSERTS

Desserts (Great Taste—Low Fat) by Time Life Books, 1997, $14.95. Low-fat recipes for the family and for entertaining.

The Healthy Oven Baking Book: Delicious Bake-from-Scratch Desserts with Less Fat and Lots of Flavor by Sarah Phillips; Doubleday, 1999, $17.95. More than 125 recipes for reduced-fat muffins, coffee cakes, pancakes, scones, pies, layer cakes, cheesecakes, cookies, and more.

Let Them Eat Cake: 140 Sinfully Rich Desserts—with a Fraction of the Fat by Susan Gold Purdy; William Morrow, 1997, $25. Each recipe includes the author's explanation of how she cut the fat from the traditional versions.

HOLIDAYS AND ENTERTAINING

Desserts (Great Taste—Low Fat). See description above under Baking and Desserts.

Entertaining Light: Healthy Company Menus with Great Style by Martha Rose Shulman; Bantam Books, 1991, $29.95. Three hundred recipes for every occasion, from intimate dinners to large cocktail parties.

Holiday Cooking (Great Taste—Low Fat) by Time-Life Books, 1996, $14.95. Make traditional holiday feasts with all the trimmings, but with 30 percent or less in fat calories.

CALORIE COUNTS/FOOD COMPOSITION

The American Diabetes Association Guide to Healthy Restaurant Eating by Hope Warshaw; ADA, 1998, $13.95. Analyses of more than 2,500 items from nearly sixty of the most popular restaurant chains in the U.S.

Bowes and Church's Food Values of Portions Commonly Used (17th edition) by Jean A.T. Pennington; Lippincott-Raven, 1997, $36. More than 8,500 common foods and their nutritional contents, organized by food groups.

Calories and Carbohydrates (13th edition) by Barbara Kraus; Signet Books, 1999, $6.99. More than 8,500 brand-name and basic foods with their calorie and carbohydrate counts.

The Complete Book of Food Counts (4th Edition) by Corinne T. Netzer; Dell, 1999, $7.50. Thousands of brand-name and basic foods analyzed for their calories, carbohydrates, cholesterol, sodium, protein, fat, and fiber.

Eating Out Food Counter by Annette Natow and Jo-Ann Heslin; Pocket Books, 1998, $6.99. The data on away-from-home meals, from breakfast to late-night snacks.

RECOMMENDED MAGAZINES

Give yourself a monthly boost of support plus a host of recipes and other ideas from these magazines that promote a healthy lifestyle:

Better Homes & Gardens, 1716 Locust St., Des Moines, IA 50309. Subscriptions: (800) 374-4244

Cooking Light, P.O. Box 1748, Birmingham, AL 35201. Subscriptions: (800) 336-0125

Fitness, 375 Lexington Ave., New York, NY 10017. Subscriptions: (800) 888-1181

Good Housekeeping, 959 Eighth Ave., New York, NY 10019. Subscriptions: (800) 888-7788

Health, 2 Embarcadero Center, #600, San Francisco, CA 94111. Subscriptions: (800) 274-2522

Prevention, 33 East Minor St., Emmaus, PA 18098. Subscriptions: (800) 914-9363

Self, 4 Times Square, 5th floor, New York, NY 10036. Subscriptions: (800) 274-6111

Shape, 21100 Erwin St., Woodland Hills, CA 91367. Subscriptions: (800) 340-8953

RECOMMENDED NEWSLETTERS

What's the major difference between magazines and newsletters? Advertisements—newsletters usually don't have any, and that's why they're more expensive than magazines. Also, newsletters cut right to the chase . . . no fashion, beauty, or relationship advice, for example—just solid reporting on research and practical advice on how to use the findings in your everyday life. Most of the newsletters we list below are sponsored by universities or government organizations and are not devoted solely to nutrition, weight management, or fitness. Nevertheless, those are major topics in every one of them, and each also has the reputation for stringent standards for accuracy.

Consumer Reports on Health, P.O. Box 56360, Boulder, CO 80323. Subscriptions: (800) 234-1645. From the people who bring you the highly respected *Consumer Reports* magazine.

Environmental Nutrition, 2112 Broadway, Suite 200, New York, NY 10023. Subscriptions: (800) 829-5384. Covers a wide range of nutrition topics; all authors are registered dietitians.

FDA Consumer, Superintendent of Documents, P.O. Box 371954, Pittsburgh, PA 15250. Subscriptions: (202) 512-1800. This official publication of the U.S. Food and Drug Administration offers a wealth of new and in-depth info on how to get healthy and stay healthy and reports on cases that illustrate FDA actions to protect the public from unsafe products.

Harvard Health Letter, P.O. Box 420235, Palm Coast, FL 32142. Subscriptions: (800) 829-9045. Big on patient advocacy, encouraging readers to take greater responsibility for the management of their own health and their dealings with medical professionals.

Harvard Women's Health Watch, P.O. Box 420235, Palm Coast, FL 32142. Subscriptions: (800) 829-5921. Provides the latest news about women's health and seeks to clarify many of the issues with concise, accurate information. Subjects range from hormone replacement therapy to weight management to heart disease.

Mayo Clinic Health Letter, P.O. Box 53886, Boulder, CO 80322. Subscriptions: (800) 666-3703. Draws on the expertise of more than 1,100 Mayo Clinic physicians on nutrition and healthy eating, new medical treatments, and more.

Mayo Clinic Women's HealthSource, P.O. Box 56931, Boulder, CO 80322. Subscriptions: (800) 678-5481. Prevention and treatment of disease, plus medical research, nutrition and weight control info, and lifestyle issues such as exercise and stress management.

Tufts University Health & Nutrition Letter, P.O. Box 420235, Palm Coast, FL 32142. Subscriptions: (800) 274-7581. Takes the science out of labs and brings it into people's lives for use in their kitchens, supermarkets, medicine cabinets, and doctors' offices.

Women's Health Advocate Newsletter, 7811 Montrose Rd., Potomac, MD 20854. Subscriptions: (800) 829-5921. Helps women understand their health choices, talk to their doctors, and make informed decisions about preventing disease and increasing their energy and vitality.

University of California at Berkeley Wellness Letter, P.O. Box 420235, Palm Coast, FL 32142. Subscriptions: (800) 829-9080. Nutrition, fitness, and stress management are major topics.

OUR FAVORITE WEBSITES

The following have solid, accurate information about dieting, and/or nutrition and calorie counts, and/or fitness. All have links to additional sources of reliable information.

American Dietetic Association http://www.eatright.org. Click on Nutrition Resources, then on Nutrition Fact Sheets.

CyberDiet http://www.cyberdiet.com. Provides a personalized diet profile and aids you in planning your daily food intake.

Mayo Clinic's "Health Oasis" http://mayohealth.org. Click on Nutrition Center.

Minnesota Attorney General's Office "Fast Food Facts" http://www.olen.com/food. Covers menu items from many of the most popular American chains.

National Heart, Lung, and Blood Institute http://www. nhlbi.nih.gov. Click on Achieving Your Healthy Weight.

Shape Up America http://www.shapeup.org. Especially click on Cyberkitchen.

U.S. Department of Agriculture's Food and Nutrition Information Center http://www.nal.usda.gov.fnic. Covers 100 nutrients for 7,300 foods.

U.S. Food and Drug Administration's Center for Food Safety and Applied Nutrition http://vm.cfsan.fda.gov. Click on Special Interest Areas: Women's Health, then on Losing Weight and Maintaining a Healthy Weight.

University of Illinois' Nutrition Analysis Tool http://www.ag.uiuc.edu/~food-lab/nat. Calculates calories and nutrients for almost anything you can think of.

OTHER GOOD WEB STUFF

Recipes Online

http://www.epicurious.com
http://www.kitchenlink.com
http://www.baychef.com
http://www.foodwine.com
http://www.mastercook.com
http://www.cyber-kitchen.com
http://www.foodstuff.com

Devoted Specifically to Low-Fat Recipes and Living

http://www.cookinglight.com
http://www.fatfree.com

Miscellaneous

http://www.VRG.org; Website of the Vegetarian Resource Group
http://www.caloriecontrol.org; information about weight management and food trends

Exercise

http://www.aceFitness.org
http://www.cooperaerobics.com

HELPFUL SOFTWARE

"DietPower" is designed to help you lose weight, improve your vitamin and mineral intake, and keep track of your exercise and calorie-burning. Call (800) 852-8446 for more information.

FOOD, FUN, FOREPLAY, AND FACTS ON THE RADIO

Ellen Albertson is a dietitian. Her husband Michael Albertson is a chef. Put them together and they're "The Cooking Couple" who created two syndicated radio shows. *Food as Foreplay*, which has been described as part call-in therapy and part recipe wrangling and is designed to help couples improve their relationships through food. "If a couple's not getting along in the kitchen," Ellen has said, "then they're probably not getting along in other aspects of their life." Their other show—*Cooking Couple's Kitchen*—is more family-friendly. To find out if a radio station in your area broadcasts either or both, visit http://www.cookingcouple.com.

CHAPTER NINE

COPING WITH STRESS . . .
AND ITS PHYSICAL
SOUVENIRS

*L*etters from nervous brides-to-be with knotty family problems are a staple of advice columns. Dear Abby, for example, recently counseled one bride-elect whose stepmother insisted on being included in all of the wedding plans "not because we are particularly close," the letter writer lamented, "but to show her 'socially elite' friends what a wonderful wedding *she* threw, even though she and my father refuse to pay for anything."

That same week, Abby dealt with a prospective bride whose mother insisted she provide a complete list of the wedding gifts

she was receiving so that "Mother will know for future reference what to give the gift givers in return," wrote the bride.

Not long after, a horrified Miss Manners fielded a letter from a distraught young woman whose fiancé planned to place a large ceramic turtle at the front door of their wedding reception. Further, the guy intended to attach a sign reading NO BILLS LESS THAN $20 near a slot in the turtle's shell. "I am appalled," the woman wrote. "He claims it is a common practice, used to contribute to the bride and groom's honeymoon, or for those who did not have time to buy a gift."

These are extreme examples, but since a wedding is an emotionally charged event—and traditions, expectations, and other factors vary among families—you should anticipate at least some family squabbling and stepped-on toes before the big day arrives (for help, see the sidebar Ten Ways to Argue More Productively).

What it boils down to is the potential for more stress on top of the stress you may already be feeling as you run around taking care of the myriad tasks involved in putting on a wedding and reception. Too much stress can affect not just your mood, mental state, and energy level, but your looks, as well—by producing a new crop of pimples, for example, or robbing you of restful sleep (read: bags and dark circles). Later in this chapter, we'll help you deal with those stress souvenirs. For now, however, here's a pound of prevention. There are dozens of ways to decrease and manage stress:

Talk to yourself: If you can't avoid a stressful situation, try to calmly put your negative feelings into words, such as "I'm upset because I'm stuck in traffic and I have a hundred things to do." Then try to come up with at least three ways to make the situation more tolerable, such as 1) I can get off the freeway and take Sepulveda instead; 2) I can buy a birthday cake for my coworker instead of baking one; 3) I can call Mom and ask her to meet me at the bridal salon rather than picking her up.

Use humor: Stresscare, a Long Island, New York, firm that conducts stress management seminars, recommends the "blow-up" method of diffusing a stressful situation. You mentally blow a situation all out of proportion until it's ludicrous . . . and funny. If it looks like you will be late meeting the wedding coordinator at your church, you could tell yourself, "My husband-to-be will have to meet her alone. Even though she is forty years older than he is, they will fall madly in love at first sight. He will spurn me and marry her, and I will try to maintain at least a friendly relationship with him through the years by helping him clean her dentures, oil her wheelchair, and cook her custards and Jell-O until she dies and I can have him back."

Think of delays as opportunities: There are fifteen people in front of you at the passport office and you have to be some-

Ten Ways to Argue More Productively

Uh-oh. You and your mother/father/fiancé/future in-law don't see eye to eye about some aspect of your wedding/reception/honeymoon. The following tips from communication skills consultant Audrey Nelson-Schneider, Ph.D., will keep the conflict from escalating and will hasten a resolution.

• **Allow time for anger and hostility to be expressed.** This gets the real issues right out front and enables you to better manage the rest of the conflict.

• **Begin on points of agreement—don't polarize.** Example: "We both want to have the most beautiful wedding possible within our budget."

• **Remind the other person of such mutual interests throughout the conflict.**

• **Don't deny the other person his/her feelings.** Don't say "Jason, you have no right to be angry that I won't let you put that ceramic turtle on the front porch. It's an atrocious idea!"

• **Actively listen to the other person.** Don't just be thinking up your next rebuttal.

• **Focus on the other person's interests.** Read between his/her lines. Is your stepmother upset that you won't use her friend, the caterer, or is she really just resentful that you're not giving her a larger role in planning the wedding?

• **State empathy whenever you feel it.** Example: "Dad, I'd feel hurt, too, if my daughter walked down the aisle with her stepfather, like Mom wants. So I've come up with a compromise. . . ."

• **Demonstrate your willingness to see his/her side.** If you've really been trying to empathize throughout the conflict, it will be easier to see his/her side. Example: "Jason, I can understand why you want people to put big bucks in that turtle—we sure could use them in our condo downpayment fund. But among my friends and family, such a blatant plea for cash is a turn off, because they consider it. . . ."

• **Agree with the other person when possible.** Even add to his/her argument. "I can certainly understand why you want to go with Acme Photography, Mom. You know them well, and you've had no time to research any other firms—not when you've been putting in sixty-hour weeks at work! But I have had the time to do some research, and I am really impressed with. . . ."

• **Use "I" statements instead of "you" statements.** Don't say, "Mom, this is my wedding and you should stop feeling sorry for yourself and stop butting in!" Instead: "I can understand why there are hard feelings between you and my stepmother, Mom. And though she could never take your place in my heart, she has been loving and giving to me these past ten years, so I feel she deserves to sit in the first row, too."

where in twenty minutes. Always stash something constructive to do in your bag, be it proofreading your wedding announcement for the newspaper, browsing library books for potential wedding readings, or writing thank-you notes for shower gifts.

Make lists—but set priorities: It's a good idea to make a list each day of things that need to be done. But such a list can be overwhelming if it gets too long. Solution: Organize the list by making the first task the one that has the highest penalty should you be late in doing it; the second item has the next-worst penalty, and so on. For example, the penalty if you don't "FedEx Mom's birthday gift" is probably greater than the twenty-five cents you'll have to pay if you fail to "Return the library book due today."

Set up a budget—then stick to it: Money is a major source of stress in life, and weddings are a major expense. You can save yourself a lot of worry and head off arguments by sitting down with everybody who is contributing financially to the wedding and drawing up a budget—this much for flowers, this much for photography, etc. If you need help, we recommend two books by budgeting expert Judy Lawrence: *The Budget Kit: The Common Sense Money Management Workbook* (Dearborn Trade, 1997) and *The Money Tracker: A Quick and Easy Way to Keep Tabs on Your Spending* (Dearborn Trade, 1996).

Delegate! Gone are the days when the groom-to-be's role was simply to show up at the church on time. Lots of brides we know made their husbands-to-be completely responsible for planning the honeymoon or for making all music arrangements for the wedding and reception or for ensuring that all the groomsmen were properly attired. Ten to one, you'll be doing the lion's share of the work necessary for the wedding and reception, but to let him get off scot-free is setting a bad precedent! After all, do you want to be doing all the cooking *and* all the dish washing after you're married?

Family and friends will no doubt be pleased and flattered if you seek their help. But expect some resentment if the only chores you'll delegate are the grunt ones. If you assign your mother the tedious task of locating and reserving hotel rooms for out-of-towners, take her along and seek her input when you go to the florist.

Lower your standards: Creating a wedding and reception will often feel like a full-time job. And that's on top of the full-time job you've already got. Something's got to go, and in the weeks or months before your wedding, let that be something other than your wedding or your career. You will not be arrested if your apartment isn't fastidiously neat or your nail polish is chipped.

Learn to say no: It seems to be a law of the universe that whenever you are frantically busy, the needs of your friends, family, and coworkers increase proportionately. Your office mates are pushing you to organize the annual employee picnic. Your child's room mother wants you to bake two dozen cupcakes for the Valentine's Day party. Your best friend asks you to baby-sit her two toddlers while she and hubby weekend somewhere. You can effectively refuse without resorting to a scream of "No! No way! Absolutely positively *not!*" Just say in a harried, semihysterical, somewhat breathless voice, "Look, I wish I could help but I can't. I'm simply overwhelmed." Leave what you're overwhelmed by to the requester's imagination. You really don't owe anyone an explanation for saying no to a request for your time, especially if you know darn well that saying yes is going to make your life even crazier.

Stress management experts advise asking yourself a handful of questions before saying yes to a request for your time: Do I *have* to do this? Will I enjoy doing it? Is this project important to me? Do I have the energy and time to do it? If you answer no to any of these questions, seriously consider making that your final answer.

If you're Polly Pleaser and can't bring yourself to say an outright no, buy yourself time: "I'll have to check my schedule and get back to you." Not only will this prevent you from saying yes because you were caught off-guard, it will also give you the opportunity to come up with an excuse for not accepting the person's request if you don't want to do it. You can then call the person back and say, "I'm sorry, but I checked my schedule and I'm busy that day." And that's no lie! Because during this time of your life, you're busy *every* day.

Give yourself a pep talk: A lot of stress is self-inflicted, thanks to the negative and often self-deprecating comments we make when we're talking to ourselves, such as, "There's no way I can finish everything I have to do." Wrest yourself out of this state by overriding such thoughts with positive ones, such as "I've accomplished a lot today!"

Pet your pet: University of Maryland researcher James Lynch conducted a study in which he found that just petting your dog or cat is a natural stress reliever. It slows your heart rate and lowers your blood pressure.

Pop bubbles: This is another somewhat off-the-wall suggestion, but believe us—it works! A few years ago, researchers at Western New England College in Springfield, Massachusetts—yes, somebody actually did a study on this—found that students were less tense and more calm and energized after popping sheets of bubble wrap. That's the plastic packing material with sealed-air capsules that you'll be getting reams of, once the wedding gifts start to arrive in the mail. Kathleen Dillon, Ph.D., the professor of psychology who directed the study, said that popping the plastic bubbles is in the same league as knitting, finger tapping, and fiddling with worry beads—all activities that dispel muscle tension and pent-up nervous energy. She added that bubble popping has advantages over more conventional de-stressing techniques, such as meditation, because no instruction or practice is required to achieve satisfactory results. By the way, study participants preferred popping the larger bubbles over the smaller variety—"a more satisfying pop," was the general consensus.

Go for a walk: A brisk, fifteen-minute walk has been found to be more calming than some tranquilizers. And regular walking—actually, regular exercise of any kind—helps the body adapt more readily to stress. A fit body pumps out lesser amounts of the "fight or flight" hormones that produce stress symptoms such as sweating.

Don't bottle up your emotions: According to the authors of the book *The Stress Solution*, repressing anger, anxiety, or depression decreases your resistance to stress. Get things off your chest. Having at least one close, trusted friend to confide in is also important. According to one study, women who are under severe stress and don't have somebody to confide in are twice as likely to be depressed as women who are equally stressed but who have a confidante.

Schedule a music break: Researchers say that playing calm music in the operating room reduces a patient's anesthesia needs, because it has a tranquilizing effect. Whenever you have even a few minutes to spare, turn on your stereo and just sit, relax, and listen. No rock, rap, or metal, please. You don't have to resort to "elevator music," but do opt for something slow, nonvocal, and quiet for best results. A woman we know, the mother of two hormonally berserk teens, swears by Pachelbel's "Canon in D Major." "Canons," she says, "are mesmerizing."

Try a relaxation exercise:

Here are three that we especially recommend:

• *Visual imagery.* Close your eyes and revisit the most relaxing place you've ever been to. Manufacture every vivid detail you recall—the feel of the sun on your back, the hissing of the ocean, and so on. Try to stay in that place for at least five minutes.

• *Progressive muscle relaxation.* The principle: A muscle will relax automatically after it is tightened forcefully. Lie on your back and concentrate on tightening your forehead for five seconds, then relax it. Progress down your body, one part at a time, tightening and relaxing your jaw, neck, shoulders, all the way down to your toes. Try to set aside at least fifteen minutes for this exercise.

• *The Relaxation Response.* Harvard researcher Herbert Benson devised this exercise because his studies showed that when people meditate, a feeling of tranquillity washes over them. In turn, muscle tension, heart rate, brain-wave activity, and blood pressure decrease. All you need is a quiet part of your home (even a closet, if necessary) and at least ten but preferably twenty uninterrupted moments. Close your eyes and repeat silently a meaningless word or phrase—you may wish to use the universal mantra "om"—over and over again. Try to concentrate on that sound only. If an intrusive thought drifts in, say "Oh, well," and let it go. Then return to your mantra.

Make your sleep as restful as possible: As your wedding day comes closer, you may find that the amount of sleep you're getting is decreasing proportionately, what with late-night bachelorette partying, relatives camping out in your living room, etc. You need an adequate amount of sleep not just to maintain a high energy level and a good mood, but also to ensure a fresh, rested look—one devoid of bleary eyes, bags, and circles.

You may not be able to get the quantity of sleep you need, but you can improve the quality. Sleep researchers break the sleep cycle down into stages. The deepest, most restful sleep is found in stages three and four. To get to those stages and remain in them long enough to receive their restorative qualities, make your sleep conditions as optimal as possible. Here are tips from sleep experts:

- *Cut back on drinking.* Alcohol does make it easier to fall asleep, but it also tends to make sleep lighter throughout the rest of the night.
- *Exercise to ensure that your body will be as tired as your mind is at night.* Do your exercising, however, as early in the day as possible, and certainly before dinner. Late-day exercising may make you feel too wired to fall asleep.
- *Make yours a tranquil sleep environment.* Your bedroom should be dark, quiet, and at a comfortable temperature (most people sleep best when the room is between 60 and 65 degrees). Ask friends and family not to call you after a certain time—say, ten P.M., or turn off the ringer on your bedroom phone. Shut the windows and use a fan to keep out external noises (barking dogs, police sirens). External noises don't have to wake you up in order to disrupt your sleep. Such noises can kick you out of a deep stage of sleep and into a less restful one.
- *Limit your caffeine intake.* You don't have to cut out caffeine entirely, but if you're having trouble falling asleep or staying asleep, start by cutting back in the afternoon and evening hours. Make it a rule to not have coffee, tea, or cola after four P.M. And be cautious even about decaf coffee. Four mugs of brewed decaf pack as much caffeine as a twelve-ounce cola.

If you're using caffeine as an antidote to fatigue, be aware that while it will in fact perk you up, it's only a short-term remedy. When it wears off after a couple of hours, you'll feel even more exhausted. Keep pouring it on and you risk caffeine overload, which can make you jittery and cranky. Bottom line: *Sleep* is the cure for sleepiness, not caffeine. So, if you do have the opportunity:

Take a nap or go to bed earlier: Humans are biologically wired for one nap a day—usually in the midafternoon, according to University of Ottawa researcher Roger Broughton, M.D. Studies show that napping not only will make you feel better, it will also make you better able to concentrate and to make complex decisions. The rules of napping: You need at least twenty minutes (thirty is better) but no more than one and a half hours. Shorter than twenty minutes and the nap will have no restorative benefits; go longer than ninety and it will be harder to fall asleep that night and/or your nighttime sleep will be lighter and not as restful.

Again, if you can spare the time, it's better to go to bed earlier than usual than to sleep later than normal. This is because we reset our body clocks by getting up at the same time every morning. Sleeping later than usual disrupts your body rhythms, leading to feelings of sluggishness or just a low-grade yuckiness during the day. Going to bed early to make up for lost sleep has no side effects.

VITAMINS FOR STRESS

You can't live in the real world and avoid every bug that comes around. But you can strengthen your immune system—your bug-fighting defenses—so that you're less likely to be suffering from a cold or other such nuisance on your wedding day. Begin taking a multivitamin three months before the wedding. Take a basic, low-cost multivitamin— you don't need a "stress formula" or one that's loaded with minerals or special herbs and botanicals. Foodwise, you want to make sure you're getting enough of the following vitamins and minerals in your diet, because they're the ones most responsible for a healthy immune system:

• *Vitamin C.* The daily recommended dosage is 60 mgs., but 200 mgs. is a better bet, and you may need to buy a supplement to get to that level. Take any more than that, however, and it will simply pass out of your body in the urine. Good food sources: oranges, orange juice, grapefruit, grape-fruit juice, strawberries, cantaloupe, red bell peppers, broc-coli, kiwifruit, and brussels sprouts.

• *Vitamin B 6.* Besides transforming food into energy and ensuring healthy function of nerve tissue, B 6 is believed by scientists to help strengthen the immune system. You should get all 1.3 mgs. you need per day through food, not supplements, because long-term use of supplements—of, say, 200 mgs. a day—can cause permanent nerve damage. Foods that are rich in B 6 include salmon, watermelon, potatoes, brown rice, avocados, turkey, chicken, and bananas.

• *Zinc.* Many women are lacking in this immune-system builder, but supplements aren't recommended because excess zinc can inhibit the absorption of copper, another vital nutrient. Instead, strive to get the recommended daily allowance of 15 mgs. through food sources, such as split peas, lean beef, steamed oysters, shrimp, canned crab meat, wheat germ, roast turkey, and black-eyed peas.

HERBS FOR STRESS

There are some herbal products that can help the body deal with stress. If you're taking other medications, or are planning to get pregnant soon after your wedding, check with your doctor first.

• *Passion flower.* Taken as an herbal tea, passion flower eases nervous agitation, mild insomnia, and nervous stomach. Your daily dose should be 4 to 8 mgs., divided among a cup of tea at each meal and one before bedtime.

• *St. John's Wort.* Taken as a capsule or tincture, it acts as a mild sedative for anxiety, depressive moods, and inflammation of the skin. Your daily dose should be 2 to 4 grams or 0.3% total hypericin.

- *Valerian.* Drink it in tea form to relieve restlessness, sleeping disorders, nervous conditions, mental strain, and lack of concentration. Your daily dose should be 15 mgs., split among three or four cups of tea. Valerian is the most widely used sedative in Europe, outselling all prescription tranquilizers.

STRESS-REDUCING BEAUTY TREATMENTS

The week before your wedding, several superb stress-busters can be employed:

- *Total body massage.* To unwind, schedule one four to five days before the big day—and why not schedule one for your groom, as well?
- *Hydrotherapy and aromatherapy.* These are relaxing options if massage is not your thing.
- *Exfoliation, body scrub, mud pack, paraffin treatment, and waxing.* Some of these—ouch!—may only reduce the stress you feel about your looks! Schedule such treatments three to four days before the wedding so that any redness they cause will disappear.
- *Facial.* In this case, too, you should build in at least three or four days before the wedding. That's so any flare-ups the facial may produce will subside.

• *Pre-tanning.* Tanning is not a healthy thing to do, but if you insist . . . plan to get your color in three short sessions the week before your wedding. Or try the new sunless treatments at salons.

• *Manicure, pedicure, brow-shaping.* For best results, schedule these treatments for two days before the wedding.

HOW TO FOIL MOTHER NATURE

Stress leaves its marks. Here's how to minimize them.

When the eyes have it . . . puffiness and/or dark circles, that is. The skin around the eyes is the thinnest and most sensitive on the body. That's why the eyes reveal change so readily. **Puffiness** can occur when the muscles under the eye sag from fatigue or when the body retains too much water. Other causes: excessive salt intake, an increase in progesterone (the female hormone responsible for premenstrual bloat), or an allergic reaction to eye creams.

Many people wake up with puffy eyes after sleeping on their stomachs because that position allows fluid to gather in the loose skin around the eyes. The pull of gravity helps drain the fluid as the day progresses, but you can help avert morning eye puffiness by sleeping with your head propped on an extra pillow. Other ways to minimize puffiness: Put your head back and place cold compresses, wet chamomile tea bags, or cucumber slices over your closed eyes for fifteen minutes. Ponds, the skin care company, even markets fake cucumber slices for this purpose.

We have **dark circles** because the skin below our eyes is more darkly pigmented than that of our cheeks, so our eyes appear to have shadows under them. Also, the thinness of the skin under the eyes allows the blood vessels to show through, adding to the shadowy effect. The degree of the skin's transparency is largely hereditary, but fatigue can contribute to the appearance of dark circles by causing the blood vessels to swell and come closer to the skin's surface.

Besides getting adequate sleep, the only real "solution" for dark circles is camouflage. A friend—who insists that she's had very dark circles since birth—gave us her camouflage technique, and believe us, it works, because we've seen her with and without makeup. She applies a yellow concealer stick to the circles, covers that with her regular foundation, and follows up with a second concealer product that is as close a match as possible to the color of the skin on the rest of her face.

Cold sores, also known as the herpes simplex virus, may also occur. It's a no-brainer that you need to avoid the external conditions that usually trigger your outbreaks, such as too much sun. But another major trigger in many women is stress, which we hope you'll be able to decrease and manage thanks to this chapter, but that we know you won't be able to avoid entirely. Herpes is a virus—that is, antibiotics *will not* prevent a cold sore or hasten healing. There's now an *antiviral* prescription cream that studies have shown blocks the cold sore virus to help cold sores heal. According to its manufacturer, Denavir cream can be applied as soon as you feel that first tingling that a cold sore is imminent or as late as when the blister appears. How long does it take to work? According to an advertisement for the cream, "in four and a half days your face [will be] wearing a smile instead of a cold sore." More info: (888) DENAVIR or http://www.denavir.com. The stuff is kind of pricey—$30 to $35 for a two-gram tube (that's about .07 ounces) and will require a visit to your doctor or dentist for a prescription. Here are some alternatives to treating cold sores:

• *Witch hazel and rubbing alcohol.* We've heard reports that breaking a cold sore and dotting on either one of these substances helps dry up the sore and speed healing.

• *Zinc.* Some studies have demonstrated that a water-based topical zinc solution, applied as soon as you feel the tingling that a new sore is imminent, aids in speeding healing time. Zinc apparently keeps the virus from replicating.

• *Change your toothbrush.* One study showed that seven days after a toothbrush was exposed to the herpes virus, half of the virus remained, which means you can reinfect yourself. As soon as your present sore heals, throw your toothbrush away and buy a new one. Toss your toothpaste, as well, because the tube can also transmit the virus.

• *Over-the-counter cold sore remedies.* Look for one that contains phenol, a numbing agent. Some experts believe that phenol may have an antiviral effect—that is, it may kill the virus. One such brand is Campho-Phenique.

Stress throws your body out of balance and that can cause **acne.** The overproduction of hormones is what gives you zits. Some of us remember the days when acne sufferers were admonished to avoid chocolate and to scrub the face clean six or seven times a day. These "remedies" have been completely disproven by studies. In fact, washing too often can rupture plugged-up pores (the roots of acne) and turn them into pimples. There are ways, however, to head off a breakout:

• *Drink plenty of fluids.* They help the body eliminate impurities from the skin. Water, seltzer, diluted juices, milk, and noncaffeinated beverages will all help you meet your daily requirement of six to twelve glasses.

• *Antibiotics.* Pimples are the result of the bacterial infection of clogged pores. That means antibiotics can kill the bacteria and prevent a pimple from forming. Two weeks before your wedding, ask your family doctor to prescribe an oral antibiotic that is particularly effective against acne. Tetracycline is one antibiotic traditionally prescribed for this purpose and there is also a topical version available.

Taking an antibiotic will also help you ward off other bacterial infections—such as strep throat—that you may be exposed to in the last weeks before the wedding. A cold is a virus, and an antibiotic won't help combat it at all. But the antibiotic can prevent a bout with a cold's secondary infections, such as earache.

The downside of using antibiotics is that they can disturb the usual mix of bacteria that live harmlessly in your vagina . . . and that can spell Y-E-A-S-T infection. To prevent that from happening, eat a daily cup of yogurt with live cultures—that is, not frozen yogurt!—or take an acidophilus supplement.

• *The birth control pill.* If you're prone to acne and using or about to start using birth control pills, consider asking your doctor for a brand that actually helps to prevent pimples. In 1997, the FDA approved a brand called Ortho Tri-Cyclen, a low-dose version of the pill that has been shown to be as effective at preventing pimples as prescription-strength antibiotics.

• *Learn to correctly wash your face and use over-the-counter medications.* "Acne is not caused by surface oils," says Leslie Mark, M.D., a San Diego dermatologist. "It's something that's happening inside the pores." Mark recommends washing your face gently, no more than two or three times a day, with a soap that's not gritty and your fingers or a very soft clean cloth. Then spread an over-the-counter peeling/pore-unplugging agent over the entire area—not just on individual pimples. Probably the most effective and popular agent is benzoyl peroxide (one brand—Oxy 10). Besides its peeling/pore-unplugging action, it is also a peroxide, so it kills off some of the bacteria inside the pores. If you use benzoyl peroxide *regularly*—once or twice every day to the point just before visible flaking occurs—it can remove the plugs in six to twelve weeks and prevent others from forming.

- *Don't squeeze.* Yes, you've been hearing this ad nauseam since you first hit puberty, but did anybody ever explain the science behind it? Here it is: The more you squeeze clogged pores, the more they leak into the deeper layers of the skin and the bigger the inflammatory reaction (read: zit) will be. And the deeper the inflammation occurs, the more chance for scarring.

- *Get a shot.* If your wedding is within days and you wake up with one or more of those huge, cystlike pimples, see a dermatologist, who can give you hydrocortisone injections. "The cysts will go down and your skin will look great," Debra Jaliman, M.D., a New York City dermatologist, told a bride-to-be in *Fitness* magazine. "But it's not a long-term solution."

- *Toothpaste?* Finally, an American supermodel recently told a *People* magazine reporter that when she gets a pimple she puts a dab of toothpaste on it before she goes to bed. In the morning, she says, most of the inflammation and all of the redness are gone. Weird—but worth a try if you're desperate.

Irritable bowel syndrome is characterized by frequent loose stools and gas—or by alternating bouts of constipation and diarrhea. This irritating condition is twice as common in women as in men and usually begins in early adulthood. It is almost always brought on or aggravated by stress. If you're prone to IBS and have a pre-wedding bout, try drinking three mugs of hot peppermint tea every day to calm down your gastrointestinal tract.

$\mathcal{C}$HAPTER $\mathcal{T}$EN

DINING ON YOUR HONEYMOON . . . AND HAPPILY EVER AFTER

*C*ongratulations! Perhaps you're reading this chapter on the plane en route to your honeymoon destination as your new husband dozes contentedly beside you. Or maybe you're already on that tropical beach, fingerprinting these pages with sunscreen.

Of course you want to make the most of your extravagant and well-deserved trip away from family and wedding consultants. But don't let it go to your hips! There's enjoying yourself, and then there's destroying yourself. Use the following tips to ensure that the figure you arrive with is the one you leave with.

HONEYMOON APPETITES

Breakfast: The lavish buffet/brunch offers everything you need for a weight-wise meal, such as cereal, fresh fruit, and yogurt . . . along with every food known to stimulate the fat cells of your body, such as croissants, bacon, and big fat omelettes and muffins. If you don't think you have the willpower to choose carefully, order a la carte from the menu—don't tempt fate.

A big breakfast eaten later in the morning should preempt the usual lunch calories. But what do you do when your tummy starts growling at four P.M. and your dinner reservations are for eight P.M.? This is when you need that fresh banana you took off the buffet, or a call to room service for vegetable crudités, or a trip to the hotel sundries shop for a bag of popcorn and a diet drink. Whatever you do, don't show up for dinner starving, or you'll just blow it there.

Lunch: Think about what you typically ate for lunch before the wedding, and try to find similar choices. When you're eating out three times a day, every meal can't be a "special" meal. Make trade-offs here that will allow you to indulge a little more at dinner.

If the only food available is the local fare of the honeymoon paradise you're visiting, it might help to simply stick to the basics. Make your midday eating a smorgasbord of fruits, vegetables, chewy grains, and calcium-rich dairy foods.

Buy some fresh fruit at an open-air market, then wash and peel it for a sweet snack along with a small carton of the local yogurt. You can also order a chunky vegetable soup or garden salad in the sidewalk cafe, top it with some freshly grated cheese, and eat it while munching on a few slender bread sticks. Or you and your new husband can pick up a small loaf of artisan bread at the neighborhood bakery and enjoy it with a chunk of cheese and a glass of wine.

Dinner: Extra calories can zap you from start to finish. There's the cocktail or wine, followed by appetizers, a first course, the entree with fresh bread and butter, and, of course, the dessert cart. If you order something at every opportunity, you're looking at a minimum of 1,500 calories for the meal. Based on what type of restaurant you're in, or what the specialties of the house are, you should plan to order just what will be most memorable. Everything on the menu cannot be your first choice. Figure out what you absolutely must have, and pass up the other options.

WORKOUTS FOR TWO

Try to maintain your new fitness level by getting some exercise every day. That doesn't mean you're limited to using the hotel fitness center. Look at all of the other fun ways to stay fit . . . together: swimming, snorkeling, bicycling, tennis, golf, hiking, horseback riding, even walking will burn calories. In fact, we know one honeymooning couple who were so entranced with the Colonial Revolutionary sites in Boston that they spent every day walking the three-mile Freedom Trail. When they returned home, the bride weighed two pounds *less* than she had on her wedding day.

And don't forget how aerobically beneficial lots of sex can be! Look at the calorie-burning potential:

SEX!								
	BODY WEIGHTS							
SEX ACTIVITY	110	123	139	150	163	176	190	203
Light effort, kissing, hugging	1.1	1.2	1.4	1.5	1.6	1.8	1.9	2.0
Moderate effort, petting, fondling	1.3	1.5	1.6	1.8	2.0	2.1	2.3	2.4
Vigorous effort, intercourse	1.5	1.7	1.8	2.0	2.2	2.4	2.6	2.7

MAINTAINING BACK ON THE MAINLAND

All of us have read the letters in advice columns in which one spouse—usually the husband—makes a complaint along the

lines of "She is *not* the woman I married. In fact, she is twice
the size of the woman I married!"

We know you want to maintain your new shape once the
honeymoon is over and you return to the real world. Helping
you do that is what the rest of this chapter is all about.

Let's start with a formula. First, decide the exact weight
at which you wish to remain—probably what you weighed
on your wedding day. Then go back to page 70 in Chapter
Four and decide how much exercise you're going to continue to do each week. Multiply the appropriate "activity
factor" by your "desired" weight. The result is the number
of calories you can consume each day without gaining
weight.

RECIPE FOR REAL LIFE: SHOP WISELY, PREPARE CREATIVELY, PORTION JUDICIOUSLY

Maintaining your desired weight will be easier if you keep
this basic truth in mind: *It is easier to control your kitchen
than to control your cravings.* In other words, if you crave
something that's not readily available in your home, you probably won't take the trouble to go to the store or the fast-food
restaurant and get it—especially if it's snowing, late at night,
and/or you have a mud mask on your face.

How to produce the right environment? First, if you haven't

already done so, set up a "slim" kitchen (go back to Chapter Eight for the details). Next, convert your husband to the healthy lifestyle—or at least make him tolerant of yours and willing to make a few changes in his own. Some suggestions:

HOISTING YOUR HUSBAND ONTO THE BANDWAGON

- Insist on brown rice, whole-wheat bread, and whole-grain cereal as your pantry staples. If he whines, let him have a box of sweetened kids' cereal once a month.

- Make part-skim or low-fat cheeses your household brands, along with fat-free milk and yogurt. He'll get used to it, especially if he has no choice. If he's a big milk drinker, a good way to wean him off of whole milk is by switching to the 2 percent milk variety the first week, 1 percent milk the second . . . and then nonfat for good!

- If hubby has a hankering for "Mom's cooking," don't try to compete. Send him home to Mom to eat. Those nostalgia meals usually represent loads of fat and calories, and you don't need the leftovers.

- Always serve a seasonal salad as a first course at home plus at least one or two additional vegetable dishes on the side. You'll both eat much less meat and pasta when there are more vegetables to fill up on.

• Bake or grill extra boneless chicken or pork cutlets and individually wrap and freeze them before the meal is served. They'll come in handy for weekend sandwiches, salad toppers, or as a fast dinner-for-one if either of you has to work late.

• While clearing the table, put the leftover vegetables in a plastic container and drizzle with light vinaigrette. Now you have a marinated vegetable salad ready for tomorrow's lunch.

• Buy quick-ripening fruit in different stages of readiness so it will be ready to eat gradually throughout the week.

• Stock up on enough fresh vegetables to use in the first three or four days after your shopping trip, then switch to frozen varieties, or make another quick trip to the supermarket midweek. Overbuying perishable foods means you get to pay for it at the beginning of the week and throw it away at the end of the week.

• Make it clear what you want your husband to surprise you with on birthdays, anniversaries, Valentine's Day: 14-carat gold jewelry, theater tickets, flowers, luxurious leather goods, perfume—anything but that dreaded five-pound box of chocolates!

• Instead of keeping gallons of it in your freezer, agree to go out for ice cream when the urge strikes. Truth is, once you're settled in for the night, you're less likely to go out for those premium calories.

- If he must have his treats, buy individually wrapped snack cakes and pastries rather than loose cookies or whole cakes. You're both less likely to mindlessly munch through a whole box when each serving is separate.

YOUR FAMILY + HIS FAMILY = DIET DOWN THE DRAIN?

The size of your extended family obviously doubles once you're married. We're hoping that in the months preceding your wedding you managed to get the support of your own side of the family in your battle to lose weight and keep it off. Now, though, you may have to contend with a whole new crop of well-meaning naysayers. Some of your husband's relatives will probably have rock-solid beliefs about food and eating steeped in decades of tradition. Or they will not have kept up with the research findings that have come to light in the last quarter century that have been nothing short of revolutionary in the world of weight management, such as the importance of counting not just calories but also fat grams.

Your husband's Great Aunt Agatha will probably continue to scold you with "It's against the law in my house to eat pumpkin pie without whipped cream" for the rest of her life. His Grandpa Ted will continue to bellow—every time you walk through his front door—"You're looking a tad puny, girl! Well, we'll fatten you up today!"

When dealing with such set-in-their-ways people—indeed, even when dealing with relatively *enlightened* people—it's important not to come off as obsessive, preachy, or strident. A friend recently confided to us that he no longer invites his brother Jon and Jon's wife Denise over for dinner. "Denise whips out her calorie guide and fat gram counter with every course," he explained "Makes the rest of us—snort, snort!—feel like hogs!"

Here are some subtler ways to spare yourself some pounds and a bad reputation while sparing others' feelings at family gatherings:

- When you're the hostess, establish your own signature style. Instead of being remembered for how much food you served, impress your guests with how beautifully you served it. Create sensational centerpieces, learn garnishing techniques, set a perfect table, illuminate your house by candlelight.

- Plan some noneating activities for the family gatherings you host. Play charades or Twister, hold mini-concerts or sing-alongs, stage photo opportunities with all the guests, interview everyone on video for a recorded family history, set aside fifteen minutes of every hour as adults-only time in the air jump (those rented inflatable things no one seems to know what to call).

- Introduce some healthy and lower-calorie alternatives to the traditional family menus, featuring Grandma's heirloom lasagna and Uncle Walt's hand-stuffed kielbasa.

Keep them all guessing what the secret ingredient is in your walnut vinaigrette dressing or curried vegetable dip and you'll always be asked to bring it again.

C O N S C I O U S N E S S   R A I S I N G   I N   T H E K I T C H E N

Whether you're cooking for the two of you, for a gathering of family and friends, or just for yourself, here are more than a dozen other subtle ways to cut calories and fat:

• Take the skin off chicken. On a half-breast of roasted chicken, removing the skin eliminates five grams of fat, which is equal to 45 calories. Avoid self-basting turkeys when buying a whole bird, then baste with broth or natural juices to save puddles of fat and calories. Look for ground poultry that is labeled "ground skinless turkey/chicken meat" or "ground turkey/chicken breast" to ensure that you're buying a poultry product in which the fatty parts of the bird have not been ground in.

• Cut the fat off meat. When you trim the fat off a three-ounce piece of broiled sirloin steak, you're also trimming off nine grams of fat and 81 calories.

• Make it your house policy to use less ground beef in meatballs, meat loaf, chili, and tacos to lower the fat and calories in those favorites. Stretch that 90 percent lean beef with ground turkey breast or soy protein.

• You're much better off if your food is baked, broiled, grilled, poached, roasted, steamed, or microwaved . . . not braised, breaded, buttered, creamed, crisped, fricasseed, fried, or sautéed (unless you sauté with little or no oil). The difference per serving between the first group of cooking methods and the second is an average of 100 to 300 calories and 10 to 30 grams of fat.

• Beware of cooking oil that is freely poured into a skillet. You may find yourself using as much as one-quarter cup of oil to cover the bottom of a twelve-inch pan with a half inch of oil. That's 500 fat calories that can be soaked up by your food. Better ideas: nonstick cookware and/or an oil sprayer. See Chapter Eight for more information.

• Spice it up. Another thing we discussed in Chapter Eight is how seasonings can really liven up low-fat, low-calorie dishes. We included a list of suggestions for stocking your spice cabinet, and you can break down that spice list into three general categories: the strong spices, with which you should use a conservative hand (such as a half teaspoon for three servings); the medium spices (say, one teaspoon for three servings); and the delicate spices, which you can sprinkle on virtually to your heart's delight. The strong spices on our list include bay leaves, curry, ginger, cayenne pepper, mustard, black pepper, rosemary, and sage. The mediums:

basil, celery flakes and seeds, cumin, dill, garlic, marjoram, oregano, tarragon, thyme, and turmeric. The delicate: parsley.

A couple of other spicy tips: dried/crumbled herbs are stronger than fresh, and powdered herbs are stronger than dried/crumbled. Write this formula on an index card and post it inside your cupboard door: *2 teaspoons fresh herbs equals 3/4 to one teaspoon crumbled or 1/4 teaspoon powdered.* Note that dried herbs need heat or an acidic medium, like vinegar, to release flavor. Salad dressing is a good place for them. Use fresh herbs in the salad itself.

And don't forget spice rubs—mixes of dry spices that you rub on meat and fish that is to be grilled, blackened, or broiled. Rubs provide intense flavor and they work well on roasted vegetables, as well. You can buy ready-made spice rubs or, once you become a little more spice friendly, make your own.

• Revise recipes that combine meat and vegetables—such as fajitas, stir-fries, and stews—by increasing the amount of vegetables by one-third and decreasing the amount of meat by one-third. No one will notice the difference.

• For recipes that require milk, replace whole milk with fat-free milk. Nonfat milk contains zero grams of fat and 80 calories per eight ounces, whereas a similar portion of whole milk contains eight grams of fat and 150 calories. For creamed soups and sauces in which a thicker consistency is necessary, replace whole milk with evaporated fat-free milk.

One half cup has 100 calories but no fat. It also has twice the protein and calcium as whole milk. Evaporated fat-free milk also comes in handy as a substitute for heavy cream in recipes.

• Reduced-fat sour cream instead of the regular version is ideal in sauces and dips since flavor and consistency are the same. Low-fat plain yogurt is another good substitute for regular sour cream in dips, but if you heat the dip, stir in a teaspoon of cornstarch per cup of yogurt to keep it from separating. Ever try replacing sour cream with plain yogurt or strained yogurt (see page 154) when you're dressing a baked potato? It tastes different but delicious.

• Be prudent with salad dressings. A USDA study found that salad dressing is the number-one source of fat in the diets of American women between the ages of nineteen and fifty. Choose pourable salad dressings rather than the spoonable type in a jar. A vinaigrette will run to the bottom of the bowl so you don't eat it all, while the creamy versions stick to every leaf of lettuce. And do try the fat-free and low-fat dressings. There are dozens of varieties—you and your hubby are sure to find ones you like. You can also use such dressings to marinate meat, to baste grilling chicken and fish, and to flavor steamed vegetables.

• Salsa! It's catching up to ketchup in popularity. Use it instead of the high-fat stuff like mayonnaise and sour cream. It's great on baked potatoes and as a "cover" for fish or chicken instead of creamy sauces. And salsa is not only low in fat—the tomatoes and other veggies make it high in nutrients, as well.

• Sauté vegetables in water, broth, wine, fruit juice, or cooking spray instead of butter or margarine, which have a whopping 11 grams of fat per tablespoon.

• Take advantage of prepackaged salad greens. If you're sliding away from your commitment to eat more greens because you're too fatigued to wash and tear up the fixin's, bags that combine various lettuce varieties—such as spinach, romaine, and escarole—are made for you. Just slice up some tomatoes or red bell peppers for color, throw in some chopped green onions, top with a low-fat or nonfat salad dressing, and you're home. (Great salad seasonings: dill and basil)

• Substitute applesauce or other pureed fruit, including the kind made for babies, for oil when you bake. Canned whole pumpkin and mashed bananas are other substitutes for oil when baking. Use twice the amount of fruit; if the recipe calls for a quarter cup of oil, for example, use a half cup of the alternative.

• Use only the whites of eggs in recipes. Two egg whites equal one whole egg. You save five grams of fat per egg yolk. Or try a fat-free egg substitute.

• When serving cooked pasta, toss in a few tablespoons of the cooking water instead of oil to prevent sticking.

Dining on Your Honeymoon . . .

If you *must* have oil, use a spray oil (once again, see Chapter Eight for more info).

• Watch out for "fat-free" foods . . . especially sugary things like donuts or cake. Don't ever believe that "fat-free" means you can eat all you want of a food. Remember: *Calories are king!*

Some fat-free foods contain even more calories than the regular versions, because manufacturers have to add sugar and other calorie-laden elements to make the food palatable without the fat. A fat-free fig cookie, for example, has twenty calories more than the regular version.

SOME FINAL PEARLS (OR SHOULD WE SAY DIAMONDS?) OF WISDOM

• Never put off until Monday a diet decision you can make today.

• Weekends count! There are fifty-two of them a year! An extra few hundred calories at each one will put you in the next dress size by year's end.

• If you add just a hundred more calories a day to your diet than you can use, you'll have eaten 36,500 extra calories by the end of the year and gained ten pounds.

• Vacations are not an escape from reality, no matter

Lifetime Weight Record

Wedding Date _____ *Wedding Day Weight* _____

    Weigh yourself on your anniversary every year and record your married weights on this record. Use the space provided to make notes of any significant changes that may have occurred in your life that year, such as the birth of a child, loss of or change in job, moving to a new home, joining a tennis league, etc. Finally, take stock of your approach to diet and exercise and comment on what you'd like to do differently in the coming year.

Date	Weight	Major Events	Self-Assessment

what the ads say. Your real body goes with you and shouldn't come back ten pounds heavier.

• Placing a mirror over the dining table, or above the kitchen sink, or on the front of the refrigerator—all places where you'll see yourself eating—will help you eat less.

We leave you with a chart on which to record your weight at every anniversary (may you still be able to fit into your wedding dress on the twenty-fifth!) . . .

. . . And our very best wishes for a happy new life together.

The Wedding Dress Diet Food and Fitness Log

Day _____   Date _____

Time	Amount	Description of Food	Special Features	Calories	Fruit	Veg	Grain	Calcium
			TOTALS:					

The Wedding Dress Diet Food and Fitness Log

Day _____ Date_____

Time	Amount	Description of Food	Special Features	Calories	Fruit	Veg	Grain	Calcium
			TOTALS:					

Aerobic Activity _____ Duration _____ Exercise Heart Rate _____

Resistance Exercises: Upper Body _____ Lower Body _____ Abs_____

Supplements taken? Yes/No   Goals reached? Yes/No

If not, what will you do differently tomorrow? _____

The Wedding Dress Diet Food and Fitness Log

Day _____ Date _____

Time	Amount	Description of Food	Special Features	Calories	Fruit	Veg	Grain	Calcium
			TOTALS:					

The Wedding Dress Diet Food and Fitness Log

Day _____   Date _____

Time	Amount	Description of Food	Special Features	Calories	Fruit	Veg	Grain	Calcium
			TOTALS:					

Aerobic Activity _____ Duration _____ Exercise Heart Rate _____

Resistance Exercises: Upper Body _____ Lower Body _____ Abs _____

Supplements taken? Yes/No   Goals reached? Yes/No

If not, what will you do differently tomorrow? _____

$\mathcal{I}_{\text{N D E X}}$

abdominal crunch, 103–5
abdominal toner, 119–20
acne, 195–98
activities:
   activity factor chart, 67, 203
   calories used per minute in, 86,
      87–97
   see also exercise
aerobic dance, 88
aerobic exercise, 63–66, 85, 86,
    115
   see also exercise
Albertson, Ellen and Michael, 174
alcohol, 187
antibiotics, 194, 195–96
aqua-running, 88
arabesque, 105
arguments, 178–79
arm measurement, 7

bakeware, 152–53
baking, 212
   cookbooks for, 166

bamboo steamers, 151
beauty treatments, stress-reducing,
    191–92
bench dips, 105
bench-stepping, 88
Benson, Herbert, 186
bicep curls, 106
bicycling, 88
   stationary, 89
birth control pills, 196
body fat, *see* fat, body
Body Mass Index (BMI), 10,
    11–12
body type, 37–38
   frame size, 7
   in H–O–A–X classification sys-
      tem, 38, 48–50, 99
   proportions and, 99
breakfast, eating away from home,
    126
   on honeymoon, 200
breathing, in resistance exercises,
    102–3, 115

INDEX